The
DISABLED
VETERAN'S
Story

To: GUNNERY SGt CAStRO

THANK YOU VERY MUCH FOR AFFORDING ME THE
PRIVILEGE OF YOUR SUPPORT AS WELL AS THE
OPPORTUNITY OF SHARING THOSE CHAPTERS IN
OUR HISTORY WITH YOU. I HOPE AS YOU READ
THESE STORIES YOU WILL APPRECIATE THE VALUE
OF THE SACRIFICES ENDURED by SO MANY
FOR THE FREEDOM WE SHARE.

PLEASE ENJOY THE READING AND FEEL
FREE TO SHARE THOSE COMPELLING STORIES
OF THE SACRIFICES WITH YOUR CIRCLE OF
FRIENDS.

ONE LOVE

Reece

7/30/19

The DISABLED VETERAN'S *Story*

THE SACRIFICES OF OUR VETERANS AND THEIR FAMILIES

MIGUEL REECE

7/30/19

CORTLAND
ROAD

MINNEAPOLIS, MN

First Printing: 2014

ISBN-13: 978-1499205732

Cortland Road
editor@cortlandroad.com

www.miguelreece.com

This book is gratefully dedicated to my granddaughter, Jasmine Janae Boatwright, whose electrifying ten-month-old smile in the recovery room after prostate cancer surgery gave me a reason for living and empowered me with a purpose to share these stories about the sacrifices and dedication made by the veterans, spouses, widows, family members, and caretakers.

Their devotion and commitment in standing guard as they kept the world safe for democracy and the root cause of freedom in the America we share should never be forgotten. Those veterans, families, and caretakers trusted me with unconditional confidence that I would champion their stories and make sure their legacies live on as the consciousness of the world.

Jasmine, I hope by the time you are an adult, a more conscious effort of a seamless accountability in ascertaining veterans' entitled benefits are a standard practice for our heroes and their families.

Miguel Reece

Contents

Contents

Despite the ultimate sacrifice of lives on the line daily with the expectation of receiving their entitled benefits, too many veterans, widows, parents, and orphans die prior to receiving a penny. What a travesty! This has been one of my greatest disappointments and saddest, most embarrassing experiences with the agency's bureaucratic system. The focus on numbers over service while many beneficiaries are dying prior to receiving their benefits is wrong. Why not truly serve those who have served with a grass-roots educational program of the legislated benefits in Title 38 of the United States Code? Perhaps, a VA staff customer-focused continuous education program and a partnership with the beneficiaries, caregivers, support organizations, and the means to qualify or quantify positive outcomes. Why not consider opportunities to explain VA benefits at assisted-living facilities, nursing homes, churches, service organizations, etc., and accept or update applications in the paperless system on-site with these communities as well, as a way to serve an older generation who may have computer phobias? Educating and streamlining within the community could address the delays in receiving entitled benefits.

Disclaimer

The intent of this nonfiction book is to honor and venerate veterans of the United States Armed Forces, as well as their families and caregivers, for the unconditional sacrifices in the freedom of this nation and in keeping the world safe for democracy. Of utmost importance is my conviction to protect the veterans' identities and confidentiality. Names of the actual persons, living or dead, have been changed. Each account is told as factually as possible, according to the memories of each participant and my understanding of their depiction.

The conclusions and opinions expressed in these stories are those of the author, cultivated in the freedom of expression. They do not necessarily reflect the official position or intent of the U.S. Department of Veterans Affairs in the service to our veterans.

The Disabled
Veteran's Story

CHAPTER ONE

A Bataan Death March Survivor

"We owe our World War II veterans—
and all our veterans—a debt we can
never fully repay."

– U. S. Representative Doc Hastings

"What do you know about the Death March of Bataan? I want the world to know of the sacrifices the Battling Bastards of Bataan—the 31st Infantry Regiment—endured," the veteran, A. J. Coleman said. "I would die for this country and the world's freedom. I love this country and I would do it all over again." It was A. J.'s way of creating an environment conducive to sharing his distinction as a World War II veteran and survivor of the Bataan Death March which started April 10, 1942, per his recollections. He admitted to having posed the same question to the medical staff, during his visit to the Tampa VA Medical Center, at his Compensation and Pension Examination meeting. During the examination, A. J. was deemed to be incompetent as a result of his orientations and inabilities. For the life of him, he could not remember what he had for breakfast, or the month of the year or the day of the week during our initial meeting. Amazingly, however, he was able to provide a precise account on the reason General King surrendered approximately 70,000–80,000 of the 31st Infantry Regiment and Filipino nationals after three months of intense fighting. He provided detailed, intimate memories of surviving the beatings, starvation, and disease, while witnessing the agonizing death of close friends during their journey, as prisoners of war, in POW camps, or on the march to those camps. "It was all in God's hands," he said. His compelling story of pride, love for country, heroic deeds, and God's will having been done, "deepened his faith in God," he explained.

When I rang the doorbell, A. J.'s son, Raymond, answered the door and said, "Welcome to our home," as he escorted me to the living room and introduced his father, who was sitting in his big black leather recliner on the other side of the table from where we sat. "This is Mr. A. J. Coleman, our father and hero, and this is our mother, Mabel," who was sitting on the veteran's right side. Raymond's spouse, Ann, was sitting at the other end of the table. The veteran said, "I am happy to see you. I know my son, Raymond, has welcomed you to our home, and as this is the type of people we are, you are welcome.

"Before we proceed any further, I have a couple of questions for you," said the veteran. "What do you know about the Death March of Bataan and why the VA deemed me incompetent?" I was clueless about the Death March and was embarrassed to admit it. But I was able to offer my opinion on what I believe the word "incompetent" represents and apologize for the usage of such a harsh word in addressing a veteran. I said, "I believe, in the medical community, the word 'incompetent' is used interchangeably with someone not being 'capable' and in the benefit part of the VA, we accept the term as someone needing assistance." I felt it was necessary to assure him the word may be misused, but the intent was what we believe to be in his best interest, as I explained, "During the physical examination, the physician concluded you may need assistance with your day-to-day activities. As a result of not remembering current events, your orientation to some things, places, times, and events could be a little off. Therefore on the side of caution, I am here to appoint someone to partner with the VA, in affording you the best quality of life possible. It is about accountability, having someone legally responsible for assisting you. You have made a difference in the world and now the government wants to make sure we are accountable to you for assistance."

The veteran acknowledged my explanation, and agreed it was his entitlement. He still found the need to convey the reason for his two questions and share his anger as to why the physician declared him incompetent. In actuality the veteran's short-term memory was poor and his capacity to manage his financial affairs definitely required assistance. Both his spouse and son confirmed the veteran's difficulties handling his financial affairs. They claimed A. J. would often add extra zeroes to the numbers on the checks when paying bills or would neglect his financial obligations. He would frequently ask the same questions over and over, and they lost count of the times he would forget his walker and fall after walking a couple of steps. A. J. said, "The doctor had no interest in what I had done during WWII or the Bataan March. It appeared as if his only concerns were my present medical condition in accordance with the checklist of questions he had to complete. The examiner was impersonal. He accused me of living in the past, without regard for my inability to avoid reliving every minute of each day in the Army. Something every day reminds me of those days."

The privilege of visiting, interviewing, and experiencing a firsthand account of a WWII POW veteran was a treasured experience, especially when he persisted in saying, "If it is the last thing I do in my life, it is not to allow the world to ever forget the Battling Bastards of Bataan. 'We had No MAMA, No PAPA, No UNCLE SAM, No PLANES, No ARTILLERY PIECES, and NOBODY GIVES a DAMN.' These were the words of one of the only U.S. war correspondents left on the islands and we have adopted it. There are not too many of us left who are able to share the feelings of being forgotten, being out of touch with the world on the Bataan Peninsula of the Philippine Island of Luzon. We were sick with malaria and dysentery, without food or ammunition to keep on fighting, and the top general lived elsewhere. It was true that General Douglas McArthur had visited Bataan from Corregidor only once during the fighting, in January 1942. The men sensed that when General MacArthur and his family left Corregidor for Australia in four battered patrol torpedo boats, we were now expendable."

The two hours initially scheduled for the field examination lasted four-and-a-half compelling hours of a living legend's life account of heroic history. I had to reschedule my other two appointments. Especially when the veteran said, "I am happy you are a Vietnam veteran and understand the experiences during a war, not like those folks at the VA Medical Center. I was born in January 1915 and you can do the math. Sharing my journey of life is limited." Right after these words were uttered, A. J. said, "Do you know the Japanese also bombed Manila, in the Philippines, on December 8, 1941, in the afternoon? I was there," he said. "The sad thing about this ordeal was the fact that the news of the attack at Pearl Harbor arrived in the Philippines sometime around 0300 hours local time which was 0800 hours Hawaii time. The story that was spread was that an Army radio operator on watch heard of the attack while listening to a California radio station, but a young cook, Private Seiff, was credited as being the first soldier at Clark Air Field to spread the news. It was reported that General MacArthur was contacted by his chief of staff while he was in the Manila Hotel penthouse about 0330 hours. It was unexpected; we were not prepared and were short-handed without the well-trained personnel to defend all of the Philippines.

"As at Pearl Harbor, American aircraft were severely damaged in the initial Japanese attack and the wave of consecutive, subsequent attacks. The simultaneous attacks on Malaya, Thailand, American-held Guam, Wake, Hong Kong, and Singapore were meant to serve as a well-calculated, morale-controlling tactic by the Japanese. Instead, about 2,000 American fighting men marched over to the province of Bataan and defended the broken lines. We were counter-attackers. When the Philippine line broke, we kicked butts, pushed the Japanese lines back, and reestablished new lines of defense. We stood our ground and held the Japanese off for approximately three months until we ran out of ammunition, food, and supplies, and became sick, with no clean water or medications. Some of the native infantrymen had a bad case of the runs. They had a million excuses to leave the front lines. While retreating, they would pass holding up two fingers in a 'V for Victory' gesture. We referred to the gesture as 'V for Vacate.' These were airmen with no planes to fly; members of a naval battalion without ships to sail; and former native policemen. Many of the men were just remotely acquainted with their rifles. The Japanese air and ground attacks on Manila and Bataan, after the air strike on Pearl Harbor, destroyed the U.S. Pacific Fleet in its home port, and crippled our resupply pipelines and air support with the blockade."

Sitting across from Mr. Coleman, observing the passion of his depiction of the chain of events in his journey, his face with an expression of pride, the courageous deeds in supporting and defending the peninsula of the Philippine island of Luzon were captivating. The anger and facial expression after the explanation of General King surrendering to the Japanese after three months of fighting was understandable. He even apologized again for being captured as a POW, claiming his unit was surrounded twenty to one, and they ran out of ammunition. A. J. must have apologized ten times during the meeting. The depth of his sentiments in articulating each moment vividly was so surreal, his spouse Mabel asked to be excused to the kitchen. This was under the pretense of having to prepare the evening supper. It was not the first time she had heard A. J.'s account of the atrocities of war, or the narrow line between life and death, was my assumption. It appeared to me the family might have heard the veteran's harrowing stories a couple of times previously. Especially when the daughter-in-law became very emotional when A. J. started saying, "The other young men and I learned to deal with inhumane treatment day after day, month after month, and I found strength outside of me. We were a group of hungry and mostly sick soldiers who gave it our best." He asked to be excused from the table for a couple of minutes so he could retrieve a copy of an old journal he had of his remembrances of World War II. He insisted on showing me a copy of this document to share with the world. A. J. said, "It is my obligation and the right thing for the world to understand and appreciate the unconditional sacrifice we, America's fighting men and our Filipino allied brothers, endured for the liberty and freedom for the world." It was very difficult to convince A. J. I could not accept his journal in my capacity as a field examiner/investigator, a government employee. He said, "Then you are my friend, family, and my brother, not a government employee. I will make you a copy to share with the world."

During A. J.'s departure from the room and Mrs. Coleman's retreat to the kitchen to prepare the evening supper, Raymond's spouse, Ann, apologized for being so emotional. She said, "I have listened, heard, felt, and mentally endured the atrocities of each day, week, and month, I actually see each minute as if I were there. I also know how much my mother-in-law hates war and what she believes it stands for. Mabel strongly opposed war and the authority of our government. I believe this is why she had to leave." Her spouse, Raymond, agreed with her line of conversation and said, "It was a rough life growing up in a religiously divided home. My mother is a devoted, practicing Jehovah's Witness and my father a Pentecostal Christian with spiritual gifts, such as, forgiveness, love, peacefulness, prophecy, and answers to prayer, and they are generally less bound to traditional forms of worship. Mother did not allow us to celebrate Christmas, Easter, or our birthday, at times, because she believes these festivals are based on non-Christian customs. She would always point out that Jesus did not ask his followers to mark his birthday. For years our social lives were compromised because of Mother's commitment to her religion. Christianity was first in our home.

We missed several school events and social activities because they were not in concert with her religion. Our dad would always remind us of the sacrifices he made for people, to be free to do the things they believed to be right, but we compromised ours to satisfy Mother. It was always Mother's way and everything in life was much better. I was unable to play sports because we played mostly on Friday nights and some on Saturday mornings. Dad worked a lot of overtime and sometimes, double shifts, so we could have the things he did not have as a child. My parents did not get married before my dad left for the war because Mother could not be a part of such a government organization. Dad did not want to be married and go off to war. He told her if she loved him, they would get married when or if he came back home."

A. J. and five of his friends volunteered for the draft. Five of the six were sent to war, and two came back alive and married two sisters. Both of them were captured in the Philippines as POWs, A. J. in the Bataan POW camp and one of his best friends, Harold, was captured thirty days later in Corregidor. Neither of them knew of each other's situation. They met three-and-a-half years later on the flight from Okinawa to Manila, after the war was over, on their way home.

A. J. found out Mabel was married after he returned home from the war. She made it clear she did not know he was still alive. His family and Mabel had no knowledge of his whereabouts for almost four years. A. J.'s mother received a telegram from the war department after a year of captivity, expressing the army's sympathy for his missing in action or possible death. This information was shared with Mabel and she presumed he had died. She had a gentleman friend who wanted to marry her. Assuming A. J. had died in combat, she accepted this man's offer with the stipulation and understanding, "if A. J. comes back home alive and still wants to marry me, I will marry him." It was not until January 27, 1944, that the United States government informed the public about the Death March. A. J. and Mabel were married six months after his return and have been married for the last 60 years with two sons and three grandchildren.

A. J. and his three-wheeled walker returned to the room with lots of documents and pictures in the basket. Among the documents was a copy of an old, worn journal he had of his remembrances of World War II. He also had several pictures of comrades from the Bataan March. There were fellow prisoners from camps they were in together, two of the three prisoners he had risked his life for, who were as close to death as anyone could be—without water on the ship to Formosa from the Philippines, and some who were on special work detail with him. Every picture had a story and he told each story in detail. He had a special way of telling a story that allowed you to feel the laughter, joy, and sadness of the moment and his sense of pride. I vividly remember him saying just before taking me on the Death March journey, how coupled with his beliefs and physical condition, he had pride in having survived it all.

A. J. said, "It was very strange, but adding to the chaos of General King surrendering, just before midnight a severe earthquake had rumbled through the area. Also on December 8, there ensued a surprise Japanese bombing raid on Clark Field, Luzon, sixty miles northwest of Manila. That raid had been as shocking and destructive as the attack nine hours earlier at Pearl Harbor, with Hawaii and the Philippines on either side of the International Date Line. Another misfortune for us in defending Bataan was the weather. It was the dry season in the Philippines, no rain, choking dust storms, temperatures above 90 degrees, and almost 100 percent humidity made for an unpleasant environment even when the enemy was not attacking us or we were reestablishing the front line. I can't forget those tropical snakes, rats, and swarming insects. You see, General MacArthur overestimated his Philippine soldiers' conditions and capabilities, and underestimated the Japanese capacity to fight."

The look on A. J.'s face was indescribable as he made it clear and apologized again for surrendering, claiming he was ordered to do so by the officers appointed over him. He said, "I would have fought on to my death. I did not want to be a prisoner. I did not ask to be a prisoner and I did not appreciate being a prisoner. Because I cannot get past thinking about something during my captivity every day, I am eager to share those moments with the world. So please share God's plan in allowing me to survive such an ordeal with the world. Let me tell you what it was like after being surrendered by General King on April 9, 1942."

A. J. had this unique way of captivating you totally into what he was talking about, by employing most of your five senses. He said, "On the night of April 9th we were ordered by the Japanese guards to sleep outdoors, which was torturous. Not knowing what to expect, the crawling creepers, the weather hot and humid, on hard dusty ground, and no comfortable way to sleep. There were lots of malicious rumors going around on what was going to happen to us all. The worst part was we were a group of starving men who were thirsty and mostly sick. It appeared as if about 80 percent of the American troops had malaria, 75 percent dysentery, maybe 35 percent beriberi, and most men had lost as much as 30 percent of their body weight during the battle in preventing the Japanese from capturing us sooner. We had no idea what was ahead. I'll never forget a sergeant saying, 'Now we have surrendered, we will survive the war, the Japanese are going to take us and put us in a prison camp. We will get fed, have water, rest, and just sit and wait out the war in accordance with the Geneva Convention law agreement.' The sergeant's beliefs couldn't save him—he was dead within three weeks after we were captured. War is not like anyone expects it to be. On April 10, 1942, we sat on the only paved road in the area for most of the day. The Japanese searched us and treated us like criminals. We were stripped of our weapons and valuables. The Japs took our wallets and jewelry. Anyone who had on a ring, they took, but I hid my ring under my tongue. They even took our dog tags. Then they began to beat us with rifle butts, sabers, and clubbed us with anything they could get their hands on. That went on for hours. They wouldn't let anybody have a drink of water or let us rest and they didn't feed us. We were told to march to Balanga, the capital of Bataan. The Japanese culture at that time reflected the view that any warrior who surrendered had no honor. The soldiers believed strongly in the honor brought by fighting to the death. The captured American and Filipino POWs from Bataan were not worthy of respect. The Japanese guards tortured the prisoners throughout the march, believing they were not committing crimes against human beings. We were put into groups of one hundred men, in columns of four, and they started marching us from Caban, April 10, 1942. This is where the march started for me and a couple of buddies, Leslie and Robert. During the march we stopped next to a creek for about ten to fifteen minutes. I was having problems with my stomach, had an accident, my pants were messed up. I jumped into the creek to clean my pants before we started marching again. The guards offered no bathroom breaks along the long march. If a prisoner had to defecate, then they had to do it while walking. The heat was terrible and it was dark when we arrived in Balanga, which turned out to be a small settlement. We stopped for the night. As usual we lay on the hard ground in the clothes we were marching in. It was very hard to sleep being so hungry, thirsty, and sick, but somehow, I got a little shut-eye. We had expected to be fed that morning, but they only cooked rice for themselves. My two buddies and I had committed to look out for each other as most of us were sick, thirsty, and hungry; but we had to keep on moving. It was obvious our starvation was a part of their master plan. By the third day into the march, most of us were so sick with malaria, dysentery, or both, it was hard for us to independently care for ourselves. Just about everyone who was successful in getting water from ponds would get very ill. If a soldier fell out, the Jap guard would either stab him with the bayonet or take the butt of the rifle and knock him down. Many of the soldiers were forced to go barefoot and hatless over the hot rocky roads in the heat. After four days without water or food, and suffering from malaria, I thought I could not go on further. I fell out for a couple of minutes until two Japanese guards came along. One took the butt of his rifle and hit me in my head a couple of times. This made me angry and the blood rushed to my head. I got up and somehow got the strength through my anger and started walking again. In retrospect, I was lucky the guards did not stab me with the bayonet or shoot me. My ears started ringing and have never stopped. After all these years my ears continue to ring every now and then.

"Marching through the small settlement of Barrios, the Japs had one well that was used to pump water. Some of the American soldiers would go off and try to get a drink of water and they would never come back. I saw with my own two brown eyes some of them being stabbed and shot. The local native Filipinos, however, took every opportunity to throw food and cigarettes to the prisoners. Toward the end of the march, cans of drinking water were left on the road where we were marching. The soldiers gratefully drank these. If any Filipino woman who snuck these items into the formation got caught, she would get her head cut off. We kept on marching to San Fernando, which took us about six or seven days and we were given a little water and some food once on the journey. When we finally arrived at San Fernando we were put into boxcars, which should have accommodated twenty-five to fifty soldiers. Instead, there were over one hundred of us herded into each boxcar, and the doors were locked. There were no sanitary arrangements and several of the POWs were suffering from diarrhea and dysentery, which made the overcrowded boxcars a nasty, stenchy nightmare. When we arrived close to our first prison camp, Camp O'Donnell, we stopped at Capiz, where we were unloaded and waited in the burning sun for several hours while they counted us. There were groups ranging from about 500 to 1,500 prisoners waiting to be marched to Camp O'Donnell. The Japanese tortured the POWs in other minor ways, such as preparing food near their halting place, and then, on some pretense of non-cooperation, taking it away. Many POWs were beaten up for no apparent reason or they were laughed at, struck, and spit upon by passing Jap soldiers and officers.

"The day we arrived at Camp O'Donnell has lived on in my head forever. As usual, we were sitting in the hot sun, not knowing what was to come. We were feeling sicker than ever, smelling like pigs, amongst other things. A Japanese officer wearing white gloves, with an interpreter said, 'We hate you

Americans—we will always hate you. You have lived in lux-
ury, you will live hard like animals and many of you will die
like unwanted animals.' These words have been ringing in
my ears every day for fifty-two years. The subsequent mental images of more than two thousand Americans dying or
dead from disease, starvation, thirst, undernourishment, and
physical abuse at this camp alone, and that officer's voice,
would not allow me but to hate Asians ever since then. Going
to a medical treatment facility for care and to be attended by
an Asian doctor, especially in our VA medical system, causes
me to have uncontrollable anxiety attacks. Those words lin-
ger in my mind and the mental images of the suffering flash
in front of me.

"Rumor had it that Camp O'Donnell would have medical care for the soldiers. It was just a rumor. Camp O'Donnell's conditions were even worse than anyone could have
imagined. It was a former Philippine army camp designed
to accommodate about 10,000 men. The Japanese crammed
55,000 survivors of the Death March into the camp. Three of
us went to the hospital area for care but there was no water
or medicine available. There were about fifty dead and other
dying soldiers every day, and they could not bury them fast
enough. Finding sufficiently healthy or capable, strong bodies for the details to handle burying those dead was hard. We
were lying on the floor next to dead or dying soldiers. I could
not stand it, so I somehow made it back to the barracks and
my two buddies stayed in the hospital area and later died."

There was a sad look on A. J.'s face when he asked in a
cracking voice, "I know you have seen people minutes after
they have died in Vietnam?" I replied that yes, I had seen a
person minutes after they had taken their last breath. And I
reflected that a couple of days prior to my visit with A. J., I

had witnessed another WWII veteran who had taken her last breath during my visit. But A. J. said, "Let me just tell you, I knew within myself, I was not going to leave this world that way and I fought not to leave like that. How did I do it? I don't know. It was not going to be in a God-forsaken place like Camp O'Donnell. Here I was, barely able to walk, too sick to march. The Lord was looking over me, because the guards did not beat or kill me. I got back to the barracks with chills and fever, shaking and swollen." Demonstrating, he used his fingers to open his eyes and said, "I could not see without pulling my eyelids open. It was about 110 degrees outside and I was shaking as if it was minus 10. I was sick with malaria, dysentery, and beriberi. I was so swollen, I could not see. But miraculously, I somehow got better without medication, except for the malaria, which I had for a couple of months afterwards. It felt as if I was going blind from the malaria and I would fall down. For some reason, if I put my head to my legs and brought it up in a short while, I would be able to see. I believe it was the gumbo rice, which I could not keep down, that finally made me better. I filled my G.I. spoon with the rice, put it in my mouth, held my hand over my mouth to keep it from coming back up, and I would finally swallow some to keep me alive for another day.

"Luckily I started feeling a little better because we were moved again. This time to Camp Cabanatuan, but by the time we got to the camp, I was so weak and sick. Without water, or food, I could not do much on my own. Two soldiers carried me to the hospital area in Camp Four, which was about six miles from the main camp. They put me into the 0 Ward, a building built with bamboo roofing and wood floors. '0' as in 'zero'. The reason it was called '0 Ward' is because it was the last place a sick soldier visited before he met his maker. This place held approximately forty-five to fifty soldiers. I was told every day, at the end of the day, there were only five or six left. The others would be moved outside of the building, waiting to be buried in one of those big holes in the burial ground. It was understood that medical supplies offered by the Philippines Red Cross were refused entry because the hospital was just a place to die. This was around June, July, August, and September and into early November 1942.

"I am proud to have this opportunity to admit, I am the first known man to walk out of the 0 Ward." The sternness on A. J.'s face and body language spoke very loudly when he said, "You," as he pointed at me, "need to understand how bad dying of thirst is, over any other death." As he goes on to explain, it is the worst feeling a human can endure. "I know because I came as close to that painful death as any human can and watched several die of thirst with the big green flies going in and out of their dry mouths. Most of them had some foam running down the side of their mouths. With severe dehydration, you are unable to sweat, urinate, or swallow; you feel breathless like someone is choking you, and you have no strength to cough. It is a form of death I would never wish on anyone. At that point, I had the thought that dying would be a better option, but there was an inner voice saying, 'with the Lord's help everything is going to be better.' I believe I lost consciousness for a couple of minutes. Our Lord and Savior Jesus Christ had a better plan for me. I am here to tell the story. It is the only answer I have for my survival during those days. The tally later was that only about 45,000 prisoners had made it out of that camp.

"In a couple weeks I got much better without medication. No more malaria, dysentery, or beriberi. We were getting water regularly and the death rate went down. The Japanese did not like milk. They brought us some evaporated milk at the hospital. We had a Catholic priest, Father Zephyr, among us and together we were assigned the job of mixing the milk for the soldiers. We gave everyone a half a cup of milk, which made them get better and they were able to go over to the duty side for work. The Father told us, 'It is with God's help we are getting better, because if it is his will for us to live, his will be done.'

"Camp Cabanatuan had three separate camps in one. I was in camp number one and got the job to chop wood for the kitchen. My health was the best it had been in a long time. I helped serve on the chow line and if any food was left over we had first choice. I was there for approximately two years and learned to appreciate burned rice. We were divided in groups of ten and if one of the ten men attempted to escape and was caught, the other nine would dig their graves and would be shot and then buried with everyone watching.

"I was transferred again to another Camp, Las Pinas, where the Japs were building an airfield with POW forced labor. The airfield was to teach Japanese pilots how to fly. I was lucky again. I was a woodchopper for the kitchen and once again, there was a big cauldron that always had burned rice in it. The work to build the airfield was so rough that men would put their left arm under the trolley that was on a small railroad track. The trolley would run over their arm, so they could not go back to work for a while. The Japs started questioning why the Americans' left arms were always hurt. I saw the Japs beat POWs until they passed out and then they would pour water on them to revive them only to beat them some more. One day during my wood-chopping duties, I heard a loud noise and my woodchopper buddy, Fred Taylor, looked up to where the Japs were practicing with their planes.

The noise we heard was our U.S. planes attacking and the Japanese guards running for shelter, but we just stood there yelling. We were hoping they could see us, but it appeared no one saw us or were able to help." The animation on his face was priceless when he said, "I only hope Fred Taylor was able to share with his family the wonderful friendship stories we had developed. We had a good time together.

"Within two weeks after the U.S. planes had attacked Las Pinas Air Field, the Japanese guards started putting all the POWs that were able to walk in the bottom of ships. We were crammed into the cargo holds, which had coal in the bottom. There were about 730 of us crammed into the hold—without room to sit down—on a voyage to Formosa. Formosa was a Portuguese colony and changed to Taiwan in 1949. We sailed on a ship called the *Banjo Maru* for thirty-nine days along with other unmarked ships full of POWs as well. On the journey to Formosa an American sub blew up one of the unmarked Japanese oil tankers that were traveling behind our vessel, and the water from the explosion came in on us. We sat in the bay for about ten days and nights with limited available water. I was much healthier than most men on the ship because I was a woodchopper. Therefore, I would help the sick and dying up the steel ladder for some water." A. J. kept shaking his head from side to side as he described this situation. He said, "I can remember vividly the look on the one man's face, how his arms were stiff and I put him on my shoulder and got him topside. When the guard was not looking, I slipped over, got a canteen cup full of water, opened his mouth and poured a couple drops in, until he swallowed it. I did this a couple of times. His eyes flickered, he moved his arms and said, 'This is first drink of water I have had in seventeen days, my name is Anderson and I am from Georgia.'

I gave him some more and he started looking much better as he described those dying-of-thirst feelings. I knew exactly what he was talking about because I lived through it in the 0 Ward. The guards caught me a couple of times, beat me, and put me back down in the hold. It did not matter, I had saved a life. While we were on the ship, when a man died of thirst and starvation they would put him on a board and dump him into the ocean.

"We pulled out of Hong Kong Harbor after those long ten days and nights, doing nothing but trying to survive, or helping others survive. A few days later the ship stopped in Formosa. It was November 1944 and we spent Christmas in Formosa. We only stayed there for three months and were loaded on another ship with unrefined salt on its way to Moji, Japan. By the time we got to Moji we were covered with body lice everywhere. So as we disembarked the Japanese soldiers sprayed us down with some type of disinfectant. Being acclimated to the hot weather and wearing Japanese WWI summer uniforms made us feel much colder. It was so cold in Japan a couple of soldiers froze to death. We did not have any heat, so we would jump up and down to keep from freezing. After three days we found ourselves in small seats on a train to Kosaka, with a stop in Tokyo, Japan. When we got off the train in Kosaka, there were six feet of snow on the ground. We had to walk five miles to an open bay barracks without heat and floor mats to sleep on."

A. J. said, "Experiencing the atrocities of the brutal Death March, surviving the battle of diseases, witnessing agonizing deaths of close friends and comrades—especially the faces of those dying of thirst, the inhumane treatment in the POW camps in the Philippines and Taiwan, along with the nightmare of thirty-nine days of cruelty on the Japanese ship of hell were nothing in comparison to the new battle. The new enemy was the cold weather and forced slave labor at the Sendal #8 POW Camp in Kosaka, Japan. It was a copper-smelting plant where we worked like dogs from sun up to sun down, and even longer at times, along with fighting with the weather and the guards' brutalities. There was snow on the top of the mountain in early September and none of us were looking forward to another winter.

"Hiroshima was so far away from our camp we never heard the blast. It was obvious something had happened because the guards brought us all in from our assigned workplace. The next day we were in the camp doing nothing other than wondering what the Japs were up to now. Later in the day some American planes flew over. It was the first time in three-and-a-half years any of us had seen an airplane with a beautiful star on its wings. I looked up, and with tears falling from my eyes, I was ashamed and did not want anyone to see me crying. As I looked around me, most of the men had tears rolling down their faces. They were tears of joy to be witnessing the sight and hope of freedom. The planes dropped leaflets informing us of the bomb they had dropped killing thousands of Japanese, and that the war would be over soon. The planes came back, dropped more leaflets with further instructions, telling us if we wanted food to put one man out in the courtyard; if we needed medications put two people, or clothing three men, out in the courtyard of the compound. We put one man out there just to get a little food into our bodies to have the strength to carry on with everything else." The look on A. J.'s face and the tone of his voice as he described this moment made every hair on my body stand at attention, especially when he said, "I only wanted to hang on to those hanging wheels on the planes as they dropped the leaflets, so these planes could take me away from this hell hole. I had paid the price for this freedom.

"In about three days all the Jap guards had turned in their empty weapons and the Japanese officer-in-charge spoke to us and said, 'The war is over and you are no longer prisoners of war, but guests of the Empire of Japan.' A few of the fellows in the camp used the colored chutes the planes dropped with our supplies, to make the flag to be flown over the camp during *Reveille*, on or about the morning of September 5, 1945. This was another tearjerker for the Americans in the camp, Old Glory flying. It was about 30 days before we actually left the camp, traveled on a train to Sendi, Japan, and met up with other Americans. It was our first happy day, just going to the hospital ship for a check-up by American medics and receiving U.S. Army uniforms to wear. Then we were moved to another ship for food galore, before leaving for Tokyo. When we got to Tokyo, we were not allowed to get off the ship. All we saw of Tokyo were the smokestacks around the city. The next morning we were marched to the airport for a flight to Okinawa, and another flight on a C-46 U.S. airplane to Manila. This is when I met my buddy, Harold, one of the six of us who joined the army together in Florida and the only other person who survived the war. He had also been a POW who had surrendered in Corregidor, a month after us. We came back home and married two sisters, became brothers-in-law and best friends."

Mabel said, "A. J. was my first love and will be my last love. He went through a lot, and we have gone through a lot, together or individually. But the saddest part of it all is the fact that he gave the world so much of himself and the VA turned their back on us." Mabel went into the other room and came back with a box full of letters she had written, with lots of other letters from all kinds of people, including buddy statements addressing his medical conditions and the need to be reinstated to the initial awarded 40 percent VA disability benefits, the amount he was awarded after his discharge from the army.

A. J. said, "I got a real good job, working for the Continental Can Company as a maintenance mechanic, with good benefits and good money. I did not need any handouts from the government. The people in the VA treated us as if we were begging for help or lying about our medical conditions. About four years after I got out of the service, I was told I had to show up for a compensation and pension examination. I did not need the harassment and I did not show up, so the VA reduced my awarded benefits to 10 percent. I did not need their handout and never bothered with them for over twenty years. My medical conditions got worse. Mabel and Harold, my good friend and brother-in-law, along with people from Mabel's church, started working on me to get my entitled benefits. With the assistance of the VFW and our state representative, I got an increase to 50 percent in 1971. But, it was not until 1990 when I turned 75 years old, that a VA doctor said, my arteriosclerotic heart disease, anxiety attacks, and PTSD along with all the other medical conditions, were service-related from having been a POW. I was then granted a 100 percent service-connected compensation, and now this VA doctor is saying I am incompetent." I then reminded him of our conversation on this issue, thanked him for his service for the world's freedom and for being a super human being with unlimited power within.

A. J. then invited me out back to the deck at the lake to watch a beautiful Florida sunset. He said, "This is where I reflect on my blessing every day, to thank God for the privilege to see the end of another. God is good and I am blessed."

His trust, and the privilege of sharing A. J.'s journey, along with his burning desire to inform others of the things these servicemen endured, and this very important part of history, allowed me to appreciate the price of world freedom even more. Writing his story is such an honor. My hope is that it will raise the consciousness of the world and captivate the awareness or remind us of the human sacrifices.

CHAPTER TWO

We Don't Need and Won't Allow the VA in Our Business

"With malice toward none, with charity for all, with firmness in the right as God gives us to see the right, let us strive on to finish the work we are in, to bind up the nation's wounds, to care for him who shall have borne the battle and for his widow, and his orphan, to do all which may achieve and cherish a just and lasting peace among ourselves and with all nations."

– PRESIDENT ABRAHAM LINCOLN

"I don't trust the government or the VA and don't want you to come to our home. If you show up at my door, I will kick your ass!" said the person who answered the phone. I replied, "Where I am from, you have to take a butt to kick a butt and I have a big butt." I also informed the person on the other end, "I will be ringing your front doorbell and knocking at your door at 0900 hours tomorrow. If I do not see you face-to-face, the money the VA owes you cannot be released and it is a sizeable amount."

Luther called me every name in book and accused me of threatening him. I assured him that the information I shared was the requirement to physically visit his residence and that to validate his identity is mandatory. I also addressed the ramped-up rage of identity theft in our society, of late. The VA is very adamant about guarding and protecting the beneficiaries from those evils and for this reason it is imperative we have a face-to-face meeting. Contrary to the local VA Regional Office policy, I contacted the veteran prior to the visit. It was understood we needed to assess the physical, mental, and social environment in the most natural state as possible. A "No Notice Visit" was our marching orders, but I was responsible for thirteen counties in the state and to drive an hour-and-a-half one way, only to find out no one was at home, is not a reasonable approach in serving the veteran. Therefore, I scheduled appointments to assure the veteran and someone else was available to have a face-to-face interview.

My predecessor, who had those thirteen counties for nineteen years, explained the importance of making the best first impression possible. He made it clear that surprising a sick veteran is not a reasonable approach. Especially when we consider the diagnosis of some of the beneficiaries we are required to visit, including schizophrenia, post-traumatic stress disorder (PTSD), bipolar disorder, major depressive disorder, memory impairment due to a stroke, substance abuse, dementia, or Alzheimer's, to name a few. The element of surprise is not a good option for either the beneficiaries or the VA representative.

I was at the local police station explaining to the officer-in-charge my concern about this Vietnam veteran with PTSD, schizophrenia, and substance abuse issues that I was scheduled to visit. My phone rang. It was my supervisor, informing me of a phone call from the veteran's spouse, Michelle, questioning who I was. Claiming I had told her spouse, Luther, "I was bringing a big butt to kick his butt; therefore, he did not sleep all night. He got dressed in his combat fatigues and was on guard duty all night." I apologized both for contacting the veteran prior to the visit and for reacting to him the way I had. My supervisor made apologies to her for my behavior and explained the requirement of a face-to-face interview to release the withheld funds of more than $81,000, which had been pending for years.

I arrived at their residence and rang the doorbell. A beautiful, warm, and welcoming lady answered the door and invited me into their home. She called out to her spouse, "Luther, the VA man is here." He said, "I am finishing my breakfast, ask him to join us here in the kitchen." I joined them both in the kitchen, introduced myself and explained to them I had a very big breakfast prior to my arrival and still had some hot tea in the government vehicle outside. I encouraged them to continue with their breakfast and apologized for not being able to join them. I was very astonished how welcoming they were. I felt worse when their special needs 15-year-old daughter, Gabby, said, "Daddy makes real, real good waffles and omelets. You should try Daddy's cooking; even the fish in the lake like Daddy's cooking." I explained to her, I had eaten a lot prior to coming to visit with her daddy and I had no room for anything else. After agreeing to go with Gabby to feed the fish when she finished breakfast, I adjourned into their living room. It was beautifully decorated, as if I was walking into a photograph in a magazine. I needed to reschedule my next appointment; I worked on the appointment letters and other required documents for this visit while they ate. Gabby was about to be picked up at 0930 hours for school, so cutting her breakfast short to take me to feed the fish was first and foremost. It was the best thing I could have ever done to create an environment ideal for opening up communications. Michelle informed me of Gabby being a change-of-life child and a blessing. I shared with her that my undergraduate degree was in education, and I had worked in special education, and could appreciate the challenges of raising a special needs child and the unconditional love she brings. She explained how Luther did not sleep last night because he also received a phone call from their 36-year-old son who had been diagnosed yesterday with schizophrenia, and Luther blamed himself for giving their son that gene. I explained to them both, I was not a doctor or a therapist, but a reasonable person. What I would do in that scenario, instead of beating myself up, would more likely be to share with my son the things I have learned about coping with the mental changes I go through, what works best for me during those hard days, or how best to eliminate them. Michelle started crying and said, "You are God's blessing to us today, despite the misunderstanding yesterday." I acknowledged her appreciation and questioned if their daughter's medical condition had been conveyed to the VA. Michelle said, "No, Luther felt it was none of the VA's business." I explained the entitlement of benefits for Gabby for the rest of her life with medical evidence showing her medical condition existed prior to her 18th birthday. Michelle said, "Gabby and I are listed as dependents on Luther's VA records." I agreed and showed them both the document I had. It showed the veteran had two dependents, but in the best interest of Gabby's future, it would be best if the VA had medical evidence showing her diagnosis prior to her 18th birthday. In actuality, the VA would not acknowledge Gabby as a helpless child until within three months prior to or after her 18th birthday. In an effort to solidify their appreciation or the extent of the value of Gabby's declaration as a helpless child, it was important they understood. If for any reason one of Luther's service-connected conditions was the cause of his demise, the helpless child will receive Dependency and Indemnity Compensation (DIC) benefits in the full amount, in addition to benefits to the spouse. This is a greater benefit and should be something to remember. I also provided them with the VA Federal Fiduciary Program Pamphlet 21-05 with quotes from Abraham Lincoln, "…to care for them who shall have borne the battle, and for his widow, and his orphan." It appeared to capture a little confidence and appreciation for the moment.

Luther was sitting at the head of the dining room table, dressed in a battle dress uniform, not saying much until his spouse starting crying and appreciating my outlook on how best to assist their son and daughter. I made it clear I had no medical training, but as a reasonable person, I thought it was best to recall his first steps and explain them with their son. It was an environment-changing opportunity, and the lines of communication opened up. Luther started engaging in the conversation. I shared one of my grandmother's old stories and happened to mention I grew up in the Canal Zone. Luther then started talking about his experience in his jungle training in Panama, before going to Vietnam. I happily explained how I did not truly appreciate growing up in Panama, one of the Seven Wonders of the World, until after visiting all those other countries in the world. It was what I had believed to be an ideal opportunity to introduce the purpose of my visit, but little did I know how deep Luther's distrust for the VA and the government was, or why.

Luther had received a letter from the Regional Office informing him the VA had deemed him incompetent for VA purposes and would appoint a fiduciary payee to assist him in managing his financial affairs. He said, "I met with a doctor for fifteen minutes and he asked about the management of the house payment, gas, water, trash, and food bills, and I told him my wife takes care of these things. Now I am incompetent. I was once the post comptroller and managed millions of dollars for the U.S. Army. I was drafted, promoted to E-5 after completing advanced individual training as a U.S. Airborne Ranger, received a Battlefield Commission, also known as Battlefield Appointment, and a BSc degree in business from the University of Maryland, and retired as a U.S. Army Captain. This is why I don't need the VA in our business. I am a proven responsible person, who had many classified missions around the world on the tip of the sword as an Airborne Ranger, working for our freedom. This doctor, a draft dodger, played the game of not going into the Armed Forces and never spent a day in a military uniform, yet has taken my freedom away after a fifteen-minute visit. I fought for his freedom and he takes my freedom away. Something is wrong with this picture."

Luther did not talk about his inability to be promoted to major, as a result of his alcoholism, which made him a victim of the reduction in force also known as an RIF. He was reverted back to an E-6, his rank before the Battlefield Commission. Luther continued the remaining last three years of his military service in the U.S. Army for retirement purposes. His retirement grade and pay were changed to his highest grade held at the effective date of his military retirement.

Luther was truly bitter, angry, and disappointed with

the VA system and defiant about having a fiduciary payee. He continued to say, "I don't need the VA in my business and I don't understand why the VA has to be this intimately involved in our lives." I asked him not to beat up the messenger, but if it were me, I would request a second opinion or go to a private doctor for another clinical opinion on his abilities to manage his financial affairs.

I also attempted to address the other question as to why the VA appears to be so intimately involved with the beneficiaries' lives. I said, "It is because so many of the veterans we visit are in deplorable, abusive, and unsafe situations. Then I related an example of a report we had of a homeless veteran with substance abuse issues, in desperate need of the VA intervention:

I only had a post office box address for him. I contacted the medical community and was able to ascertain a physical address at a church. I visited with the church officers and was very appreciative the church community had taken this veteran off the streets. He was living in one of their mobile homes on the church campus. As usual, I was required to conduct a physical evaluation of the living environment. It was not the best, but much better than living on the streets. The room in which he resided had a bunk bed and two dressers. There were lots of other little things about his living environment I addressed later with the church officers, which they did not receive well. The church officers took offense to my line of questioning about the funds' use and the veteran's needs. It was not clear to me why, when the veteran receives $2,422 monthly VA compensation, he is provided $100 weekly for incidentals; but no one wanted to address the $2,022 remaining funds. One of the church officers had the audacity to say, "Most of these funds are used for room and board." My follow-up question was "How much?" Their reply was, "We don't have to tell you and will not." I reminded them, "I represent the government and the funds you have been receiving are government funds and the government has a need to know." His reply was, "We invoke the First Amendment for separation of church and state and request you leave our premises immediately." I informed them that the VA would no longer send the veteran's funds to the listed post office box. Two days later I received a phone call informing me that this veteran had been excommunicated from the church and the VA needed to come get him by the end of the day. Not being legally astute in this matter, I wrote a report through my supervisor, to the VA Inspector General and the General Counsel, requesting assistance in rectifying this matter. I immediately contacted a professional guardian, appointed him as the legal custodian, and relocated the veteran into an assisted-living facility. The guardian, in good faith, invited him to join his family at their church and once a month would take the veteran to the local base exchange or commissary to shop. Neither the assisted-living facility nor the church provided transportation and as an army retired member, the guardian felt it was his way of giving back.

A couple of times when the guardian did not have time or was unable to provide transportation to church, he would have a member of his church family assist the veteran with transportation issues. Little did he know, this trusted, perceived church sister, a lady of God, had a hidden agenda. A divorcée, she worked odd jobs to make ends meet and now this veteran had lots of money to assist her during these hard times. Here was an opportunity she perceived to be a perfect fit in her world of survivability. She captivated his trust, dependency, and belief; it was the love he was missing in his life and they cohabitated until they were able to make arrangement for marriage. She relocated the veteran out of the county, away from the VA appointed fiduciary custodian. She then encouraged the veteran to contact the VA Regional Office and complain of the lack of support, stating the VA fiduciary payee was too far away to be attentive to his needs. In an effort to maximize her master plan, the two were married and she had control of his finances as a fiduciary spouse payee. It was not long after marriage however, before she realized how difficult it is to be the spouse payee for a disabled veteran with extreme substance abuse and PTSD issues, along with all the other secondary conditions. The struggles and efforts on a day-to-day basis are not easy; he is truly high maintenance, nothing she expected in order to gain a better life.

In addition, I was also compelled to share the visit I had with a female veteran who was a victim of designing people:

This veteran's friend, who was the VA-appointed fiduciary payee, requested to be replaced for irregularities beyond his control. One of his greatest concerns was the veteran's lack of confidence in the banking system. She kept her monthly Social Security funds of $614 and any other funds she received in a big Bible inside her closet. The veteran had a live-in roommate who had been using the veteran's funds for her personal gain. She had purchased a new BMW SUV and was freeloading off of the veteran, claiming it was the veteran's payment to her as a caretaker. The fiduciary payee also reported that her male companion had been supplying the veteran with illegal drugs, and had bought her home, valued at approximately $112,000, for only $2,000, and was now renting the veteran her own home for $1,022 a month. During my visit, I validated the aforementioned reported issues, appointed a professional guardian, disallowed the sale of her home, and directed the payee not to reimburse the $2,000 the veteran received as payment for her home. I informed her male companion that the veteran had been deemed incompetent for VA purposes, and that she is not authorized or capable in good faith of making such a sale. He declared himself to be a respected businessman in the community, loved her, and only wanted what was best for her. I then explained to him the perception of the exploitation of a disabled veteran. I also said, "Such a story in the media would not be in your best interest. Things like this have a funny way of leaking out."

After blaming everything and everyone with idle threats, he agreed to annul the purchase. The veteran claimed to see things others don't see and hear things others don't hear. She sat at her kitchen table staring forward, appeared blank, and answered questions only after conferring with her companion for validation. This case was also referred to the VA Inspector General and General Counsel's Office for their review and actions. The appointed custodian had her medically evaluated and was appointed guardian of person and property by the courts to assist her in better managing her financial affairs and life.

A spouse/payee, by the provisions of the VA manuals, has limited VA intervention. A spouse/payee can be visited by phone once every six years or by letter once every three years. It is a great avenue for abuse and misuse. In another case, the local VA Medical Center's Outreach Program team referred a case as a mental, physical, and financial abuse or misuse concern:

I was initially confused with the anger and behavior that the veteran's wife displayed with a no-notice visit. The hardest part was to watch the quadriplegic veteran sitting in his chair, enduring unnecessary verbal abuse from her while she told me that it was none of my business. Somehow he found the courage and strength to express himself in between the verbal threats. He said, "I could no longer take care of the farm or myself, I bought a mobile home and needed a park to put it in. A friend recommended this park; my wife was then the park manager. I was a widower, no children from a previous marriage, and she was divorced. Six months later she took me down to the courts and we were married. A year later she sold my 25-acre farm with the tractor and farm equipment to her son for $250, claiming I cannot use or would never be able to do anything with it. Yet she is still paying the taxes on the land out of my funds. She had purchased a van for her daughter and grandchildren, which was also being paid from my funds."

Things got worse when I questioned the veteran's fund usage and needs and she refused to address them. She said, "This is his money, I am his spouse responsible for it, and I can do what I believe to be in his best interest." I offered a clarification of her statement, by saying, "It is not his money; the funds are provided for him because there is not enough money in the world that could allow him to be the person he was when he joined the military. The funds are to afford him an opportunity to have a better quality of life under the circumstances. This is why it is called VA compensation. Being his spouse responsible for the funds are correct, but only to be spent reasonably in his best interest."

She ordered me to leave her residence immediately, at which time I told her, she will no longer receive VA funds from the Department of Veterans Affairs and a guardian will be appointed to manage the veteran's funds. This case was also referred to the VA Inspector General and General Counsel's Office for their review and actions. Unfortunately, the veteran died before a total review was completed and there was no penalty to the spouse.

It was so amazing how effective sharing those stories of the need for the VA intervention with Luther and Michelle were clearly understood and appreciated. Luther said, "I am still very dissatisfied with the things our veterans are subjected to in society after they fought for our freedom. I remember our first days and weeks in the military when the drill instructor told us to fall out, and if we had cigarettes, light them." He said, "The smokers got out of doing whatever we were doing, lit their cigarettes, and socialized with other smokers. Lots of us saw this as an opportunity to get away from work or whatever activity we were engaged in. Then later in my career during those classified missions, in our meals ready-to-eat (MRE) package, we had a small pack of cigarettes along with the food. So what did most of us do? Light them up and become addicted to cigarettes. We would often have a beer bash on the last Friday of the month, for hail, farewell, recognition, and promotions, which were understood to be a mandatory formation. After the bash is formally over, most people would adjourn to the club bar or a local bar in the community for more drinks. Some of us became alcoholics. If these are not service-connected conditions, then what is? What I understand is, if the disease was caused or aggravated by the service, then it is service connected. But the VA does not recognize these conditions as such. I may have never had a drink or smoked a cigarette if it was not a socially and politically imposed. I had some of the best ideas with both my drinking friends or during a smoke break."

He then said, "You are welcome in our home anytime,

and anytime you are in the neighborhood, please call on us. Perhaps we could have a cold one, but not while working as a VA representative." Luther appeared very comfortable he had all the time he needed to vent and I provided him with all the time he needed, despite the fact he had told me the day before, he would kick my ass.

Michelle appeared to have valued the reasons shared for the VA interventions, her spouse's concerns, and understands the need to offer assistance. But for some reason she also had the need to talk about the role of the dependents, in support of a veteran's career. She said, "Our youngest son Phillip attended seven different schools in his twelve years of school. Believe it or not, the hardest job in the military is being a military spouse. In most cases, to maintain a civil service career status, a spouse would have to accept entry-level positions as they follow their spouse around the country. They are the stabilizing force and the glue that keeps the families together. The military spouse struggles with other spouses' jealousy, and manages their homes, careers, and military social obligations. This is why it angers Luther so much to think a VA physician, who has never spent a day in a military uniform, can make such a life-changing declaration. It is not who you know, it is who speaks for you."

In most of Luther's assignments around the country, the station manager in the office where Michelle worked would contact the regional office manager or director and work out the details for her employment. She recalled their first assignment to Germany, when her career status was about to expire. Luther had visited the American Consulate, made friends with the director at the officers' club, and explained his wife's predicament. They were able to arrange her employment a day before the expiration date. The bigger challenge was traveling an hour and ten minutes each way every day and leaving the three children with their German landlord. The landlords were like parents to them and like grandparents to their children. On the weekends, after dinner with a couple of drinks, they would share their appreciation for the Americans during the war and tell such personal stories, which at times made everyone cry. Luther was on a rapid deployment team and gone quite often. She paid the bills then and continued ever since. The VA declared Luther incompetent because he was trustful and said my wife manages the household finances. "We are proud of our combined 52 years of federal service to this country and keeping the world free. The stories and life experiences shared by our landlord, their friends, and the German community, speak volumes of the world's appreciation for what America stands for and contributions to the freedom of the world." She stated, "We are blessed to have been a part of it. Luther and I defended the freedom around the world and want to keep ours."

Luther said, "I will make an appointment with my board-certified doctor and ask him to arrange a competency examination. I will then request the VA revisit this issue." I congratulated his decision for his intended approach of getting off the fiduciary program and then said I would not see the family for a follow-up visit next year.

CHAPTER THREE

The Bureaucratic Journey
of a Veteran

"The nation which forgets its defenders
will be itself forgotten."
– President Calvin Coolidge

Death has an unpredictable, sad, and very interesting way of bringing families and friends together in the celebration of the life of a loved one. The death of Henry's baby sister was no different. Her brothers, nieces, nephews, other family members, and friends from Panama, as well as other places in the world, attended the memorial service. The repast was something like a big family reunion in Ocala, Florida. Several of the attendees had not seen Henry in more than thirty-seven years. He was somewhat of an icon in our community of eighty-four families, growing up about 900 yards from the Panama Canal. Most people who knew him, would say, "Henry was in a class all by himself." He was known as a player—a ladies' man who was smoother than silk, but respected for his intellect, musical skills, and candidness.

Henry left the Panama Canal Zone to be a part of the Armed Forces he had admired very much as a child. Being a member of the United States Army was his childhood dream. He left home to achieve his vision of being well educated, a man of true integrity, and to see what the world has to offer, so he volunteered for the draft. Henry had this unconditional admiration and respect for the U.S. military members stationed in the Panama Canal Zone. Working as a package boy in the commissaries afforded him the opportunity to appreciate their quality of life. He made, what back then was lots of money, $30–40 a day in tips in 1962. Henry told the story of how he would establish trust and mutual respect with the customers and it paid well. He also visualized himself as a U.S. Army soldier away from home and appreciating what would allow him to feel at home. With those thoughts in mind, he was the best customer-focused employee. As an outstanding student in high school, a business major, whose business skills, visionary abilities, and singing talents were key elements in his success. Being a member in one of the greatest bands during the 1960s in the Canal Zone made him a very popular person around town. His perception of an education and all the other opportunities or benefits offered by the United States military had been a no-brainer for what was in his best interest.

Being the second son with five other brothers and three sisters, created a family expectation of a great future for them all in New York City after Henry had established himself. Therefore, Henry left Panama to live his dream, but his first stop was to join the U.S. Army for all the things it offers an impressionable young man.

On Henry's journey from Panama to New York there was an intermediate stop at the Miami International Airport for a layover to change planes, before going on to New York. During those days, everyone had to walk down the stairs onto the tarmac. He loved to tell about how he found fifty cents on the ground as he was walking toward the gate and believed there was money to be had everywhere in America. A couple of days after his arrival into Brooklyn, he looked up the closest military recruiting office so he could volunteer for the draft. He visited the recruiting office and met with the Army recruiter as his first step toward living his dream of becoming an American fighting man. After leaving the recruiter's office, he found a quarter on the sidewalk, which convinced him America was not only the land of the free, but a place full of opportunities and money everywhere.

The recruiter informed him of the waiting period of six to eight weeks before he would receive the draft notice in the mail, then he would be shipped to basic training. So he decided to take the subway to the unbelievable, unreal Manhattan to seek employment, which would pay his expenses while waiting for his enlistment date. Henry recalled how "it was so nice they named it twice—New York, New York." Just looking up at those buildings was something a kid from Panama could never have imagined. He wondered, "Why is everyone on the streets in such a hurry going somewhere?" Words cannot describe that precious moment in his life, he said. Wall Street, a place he had read about in the newspapers and magazines as an adolescent, was on his bucket list. Visiting the Bankers Trust on 16 Wall Street in Manhattan and applying for a job seemed like the right thing to do. He was hired and worked there until a couple of days before leaving for basic training. Henry reported to the Armed

Forces Entrance and Examination Station, Fort Hamilton, New York, at o-dark-thirty. He was administered the Armed Forces Qualification Examination, with a medical physical examination which is used for qualification or job classification and physical capabilities before entering into the Armed Forces.

Henry underwent nine weeks of basic combat training at Fort Jackson, South Carolina, followed by eight weeks advanced individual training for his Military Occupational Skills, known as his (MOS-11 Bush), and became a very proud, straitlaced Infantryman. His orders were to the historic 64th Armor Regiment, as a tank combat arms driver and maintenance specialist. This unit was known as the "Desert Rogues," the first tank unit composed entirely of black soldiers during WWII and the Korean Conflict. For some reason these orders were changed while he was at home on leave on his way to Vietnam. After reporting to Fort Lewis, Washington, for transportation to Vietnam, Henry's orders were changed again to the 2nd and 7th Infantry Division defending the Demilitarized Zone (DMZ) in the Republic of Korea. The understandable anger Henry displayed as he explained the Army's indecision of the assignment was clear. Describing his feelings during those days, as uncertain with which assignment was in his best interest, during that period in his life, is still unknown. Several of his good friends were in Vietnam and he felt left out. He had a ridiculous guilt of not being a part of going to war. He was very proud of being an infantry soldier who was well trained to fight and keep the wars off the shores of this country. Instead he played the game of watching the North Koreans while they watched him watching them at the DMZ, walking along the fence for two to three hours, with a two-hour break, then doing it all over again, until his shift was over. In winter, it felt like the coldest place in the world, which made those two-hour breaks in between shifts so important. Then the summer was hot and humid during the day but cool at night, requiring a jacket. Patrolling up and down the fence line every other day, watching them watch us, was a way of life. Henry—nor no one else he knew—had knowledge of the field being sprayed with the herbicide Agent Orange to control the growth of the two-mile terrain between them.

His guard duty walk along the fence afforded him lots of time to reflect on life. He explained how on many occasions, he would personally thank his guardian angel for protecting him from going to Vietnam and being terribly injured, getting killed, or killing others, and having to live with those thoughts for life. Those personal thoughts continued for years and years after leaving the Korean Peninsula, especially after observing the physical and mental outcome of those friends who had served in Vietnam.

At the end of his tour in Korea, Henry was offered a four-and-a-half month early out from his military obligation. Despite the love he shared for the U.S. Army or his childhood dream of being an American fighting man in the best Army in the world, the opportunity to go back to the wonderful job with Bankers Trust on Wall Street, using the G.I. Bill to go back to school and getting an education, buying a home, and starting a family were more compelling. Henry explained how he had to go back to Panama to clear his head. It was time to review his choices, which included, what was best for his siblings? Henry told everyone who would listen his stories about the bitter cold he endured in the coldest place in the world—Korea.

As a lover, Henry was known to be a player, so it was no

surprise that he shared the story of a lady in his life. The privilege of spending time with a beautiful woman after a day
at the DMZ was over and beyond expectations. It cost him
$30 per month for all the wonderful things she had done for
and with him. She gave him a Korean/English dictionary to
assist them to better communicate. He was able to speak with
her family much better, as well. His description of the caring things this wonderful Korean lady had done for him was
without question unbelievable. Marrying her was an option,
but concerns with how his family and friends would accept
her, was not something he wanted, going forward.

Another interesting story about Henry's return was his
strong conviction about the military. He spoke to the seniors
at his old high school, telling them he believed, "every young
man should volunteer for the draft or join the Armed Forces
to better understand himself or what he wanted to do with
his life." He shared his story with young men for years.

The core values the military had instilled in his life were
a perfect fit at Banker's Trust on Wall Street, Henry said. It
was a win-win situation for everyone. People appreciated
his work ethics, professional demeanor, and his acceptance
and understanding of others for the best interest of all. Being
accepted and respected in the Money Transfer Department
where trust, dependability, and reliability were a way of life in
his new work family was amazing. He had grown up so much
in that short time he spent in the military. Again, the sense of
gratitude of who he was, the choices he made and how he got
there, continued to loom every day as a moral commitment
to society.

Henry described working at Banker's Trust as feeling like
a fat cat in a cheese factory. There were so many beautiful
professional women, with such wonderful personalities; he

just did not know what to do with himself. Because if he had a fault, it was his desire or admiration for women. Henry said that his greatest pleasure in life was to please a woman. One day on his way back from lunch, he met a sophisticated, beautiful young woman on the elevator. It was very important to him to find out if she was anything like she appeared to be. So, of course, he followed her to the sixth floor and she got off the elevator and told him she had to get back to work. She said Henry was very persistent and nagged her girlfriends until one of them gave him her telephone number. Four months later they were engaged, and married six months from their first date. Sybil was born in Jamaica and educated in the United Kingdom, which spoke to her classy demeanor. His grandfather was born in Jamaica, then migrated to Panama for the construction of the Panama Canal, a man he admired and respected for his conviction. Sharing this Jamaican-born, classy lady's life was nothing more than perfect. Three years and six months later they had their first child, a son. Sybil said she stopped working in November 1973 and her son was born January 1974. She never went back to work, because her responsibilities were now to care for her family. Eighteen months later they had their daughter, now a perfect family. Henry continued to work for Bankers Trust for more than twenty-five years. On his fiftieth birthday he was given a gold watch for twenty-five years of outstanding service and later offered a retirement package he just could not refuse. The company was right-sizing and offering packages to those who were eligible. Confused and not sure what he needed to do at the young age of 51, he enrolled at the Brooklyn College under the G.I. Bill, instead of sitting at home being disappointed with life. It was a great decision, because Henry was getting paid to go back to school as he had always said he would. One of his classmates—a woman, of course—had been in the military as well, receiving her G.I. benefits, and she shared the opportunities available to veterans at the New York Police Department. She had been working there ever since her separation from the military. Henry applied for employment and was hired with the police, as an agent. It was one of the most gratifying occupations he could have fallen into at that stage of his life, he claimed. He employed his great listening skills as their counselor, advisor, facilitator, guide, or cheerleader, depending on the circumstances. He explained how he had a special gift to hear their needs, fears, and frustrations before a word was said, and for that reason he was respected and accepted.

The responsibilities of an agent demanded lots of documentation. Realizing it was affecting his eyes, he went for an eye examination. Sitting in the waiting room, he met a lady who was explaining and complaining about her spouse receiving free glasses from the VA every year, while she had to pay for hers. After the eye examination and with the information this lady provided to him, Henry visited the VFW office for assistance with his VA application. Eighteen months later, he received a letter from the Department of Veterans Affairs saying his claim for vision loss, hearing loss, tinnitus, and kidney disorder could not be validated because his records were burned in the fire at the National Records Center in St. Louis, Missouri. He was very angry and disappointed with the Veterans Benefits Administration for penalizing the veterans for something they had nothing to do with. The veterans had lived up to their responsibilities in keeping this country and the world safe for democracy, but the Benefits Administration could not protect the interest of those warriors. It was totally incomprehensible, which created a great deal of his distrust and lack of confidence in the Veterans Affairs Benefits Department.

Henry had been told that I worked for the VA, and so he sought me out during the social hour at his baby sister's funeral. His disappointment with the agency's ability to serve those who had served this country was apparent, along with his anger with what he called a "breach of commitment." He explained how he had applied for his entitled benefits in July 1997, with a denial letter after eighteen months, stating the VA National Record Center had a fire in 1973, and his records were burned along with sixteen to eighteen million records of other veterans. There were no records or evidence to support his claim, meaning no records, no evidence, of his disabilities—they had never occurred.

As he described his medical conditions and symptoms, it appeared to me to be some of the same associated with those of the exposure to Agent Orange. He also explained how he had been trained as a combat soldier, a tank combat arms driver, and maintenance specialist, who fired lots of heavy weapons during training and in the DMZ in Korea. I strongly urged Henry to reapply for his entitled benefits and provided him with the applicable forms. I also suggested a buddy statement or layman's statement, with assignment orders, performance appraisal, along with his Report of Separation, DD Form 214, and a personal statement. I explained to his spouse, Sybil, the importance of why it was also in her best interest to continue urging him to resubmit the application for VA benefits. Henry was adamant about not begging the VA for a handout, because there were other veterans with greater needs for the benefits than he had.

Henry finally resubmitted his application in January 2004, after several reminder calls from me and at the urging of Sybil. In August 2006, he received a denial letter stating there was no evidence of exposure to herbicides available for the service-connected claim for diabetes mellitus and all the other conditions associated with Agent Orange. The claim for hearing loss, tinnitus, and vision were deferred, pending a compensation and pension physical examination. Six months later he was scheduled for the compensation and pension physical examination and was granted service-connected conditions for hearing loss and tinnitus two months later. He was diagnosed with colon/rectal cancer in April 2007, which rendered him incapacitated for about six months. After numerous calls to his VA Regional Office, one of the Veterans Service Representatives explained the reason his claim had been denied was because there were no records of him serving in Vietnam and being exposed to the herbicide Agent Orange. At that point he realized the Veterans Affairs Representative and Rating Board at the Regional Office were confused for all those years in regards to how he had become exposed to Agent Orange. Therefore, Henry forwarded evidence to support his assignment to the 2nd and 7th Infantry Division defending the Republic of Korea Demilitarized Zone.

In August 2009 the VA finally conceded to the fact Henry had served in Korea along the DMZ in the designated brigade, division, and battalion deemed to be exposed to Agent Orange. It was still undetermined what type of diabetes was covered, mellitus I or II. He was scheduled for another compensation and pension examination in October 2009. By then the diabetes had gotten the best of him. He was declared legally blind, had diabetic nephropathy with chronic renal irritation, major depression, and all the other secondary conditions to the diabetes mellitus type II.

It is still incomprehensible why it took more than forty years before the VA acknowledged that Henry had been a victim of Agent Orange with the diagnosis of diabetes mellitus type II, diabetic nephropathy with chronic renal irritation, and all those other secondary conditions. These were some of the same presumptive conditions the Vietnam veterans were granted as their entitled benefit. To be victimized because of a fire at the National Personnel Records Center is totally unfair and wrong. But the saddest part of the ordeal is the fact he was granted 100 percent service-connected compensation and awarded more than $147,000 in back pay in January 2010, but was hospitalized in April and died June 20, 2010, due to renal failure without the opportunity of enjoying or appreciating his journey.

Why Couldn't I Have Died Instead of Living Like This?

"When the peace treaty is signed, the war isn't over for the veterans, or the family. It's just starting."

– Karl Marlantes, Vietnam Veteran and Author

While traveling through a rural city looking for the home of the veteran for my visit, my phone rang. A young woman on the other end identified herself as Patricia, the sister of the veteran, Richard, I was en route to visit. She said, "It is important to us all that I warn or inform you of my brother's behavior. He is angry and bitter, blames our parents for his situation, and you should not be surprised if he lashes out at you. He plays the blame game and often questions his reason for living like this instead of dying. So be prepared for his guilt trip." I extended my thanks for the advance notification and informed her how much the VA also appreciates her commitment in caring and serving our veterans.

I arrived at the home, rang the bell, and the mother Lois greeted me at the door and explained that it wasn't the best day with their son. Richard was in his room being very defiant, rebellious, displaying anger, and being loud as usual. "Richard made it clear he did not care to visit with the VA or any government employee and claimed he was not going to get out of bed," Lois said. Based on the information Patricia and Lois had shared with me, I proceeded to his room, knocked on his door, and identified myself. I said, "I am here in your best interest as a veteran who happens to work for the VA." It was an approach I have used to minimize a hostile environment. In most cases, it would create an environment conducive to information-sharing by establishing commonality.

I recalled how crazy and perhaps irresponsible I was in high school with my motorcycle, knowing Richard had become disabled as a result of a motorcycle accident. The report showed he had suffered head injuries with a spinal cord injury causing paralysis from his neck down, but was able to breathe on his own. His speech was mumbled, slurred, and somewhat difficult to understand. It was apparent to me that he could understand and reason to an extent. As a result of subsequent behavior I understood his sense of reasoning was fair.

Richard was true to form as his mother had described when he greeted me at the door. He said, "Get the hell out of my room! I want nothing to do with you, the VA, or any government agency!" In an effort to diffuse his hostility, I asked whether he had taken his medications for the day. He replied, "It is none of your f---in' business."

At this point, I had no choice but to take him to task and remind him of his military journey where respect, honor, and duty should never be compromised. I then said that I did not disrespect him and would not accept his disrespect. I was there in his best interest and if he did not welcome that, it was fine; however, he would then have to deal with the consequences of his behavior. I enlightened him of those consequences. First and foremost, if I were unable to complete this interview, his partial entitled benefits, which he had been receiving for the last nine months, would be suspended as if we were unable to locate him. I explained I had a list of questions that I needed to ask and only by addressing these to him could they be completed.

Secondly, and most importantly, as I reached in my hip pocket, and pulled out my VA identification badge, a more persuasive and compelling reason for him to comply, "I am here as a fiduciary agent of the federal government. If you refuse to speak with me, what could or might happen is that I could recommend or direct that you would be placed into a locked unit in a psych ward. Therefore the labor of love you receive from your family may not take place. In a restricted, lockdown area, the care rendered may not necessarily be a labor of love but be someone's duty, as they are just doing their job."

Somehow, these words appeared to be words of reason to him because his attitude changed. He became compliant and asked his mother to help him get dressed. Richard had been deemed incompetent for VA purposes and he had been paid VA compensation for the last nine months after waiting thirty-four months for the final adjudication on his award.

I adjourned to the living room to visit with his sister and father. At this point, his father revealed to me that his son was often angry, and had actually spit in his face because he felt his father had not manned up as head of the household. He did not elaborate and I did not question the reason for such a statement. His father left the room to assist Lois with dressing Richard. His sister, Patricia, began to explain how much Richard and his mother needed her father's assistance and the guilt her father suffers each day. She said, "Growing up, our father had a Napoleonic complex. He was unreasonable, a terrible listener, and very controlling, causing my brother to hate him. My father was cold, distant, and had unreasonable expectations for my brother. It was contrary to how he treated our baby sister and me. There was no question how much he adored us and allowed us great freedom. The girls got away with just about everything as we learned early in our childhood the right strings to pull to get our daddy to feel like a very big man.

"Therefore Richard, without an interest in understanding what makes our father tick, rebelled against our parents by joining the Army, to get away from their controlling ways. He strongly believed that if anything happened to him, our father would have to live with the guilt. He wanted to give his life for his country to torture our father. No parents want to bury their child, and Richard believed this would be a great form of punishment to both parents for how they had treated him. I believe this is why he acts the way he does. He is angry, rebellious, and nasty because he is injured and blames them for forcing him to leave as soon as he came of age. My parents have accepted blame, and have apologized to him to no avail. He has always been a rebel without a cause. Rebelling against society as he rebelled against my parents and being a nut on his motorcycle allowed this injury to happen to him," Patricia said. "The struggle has aged my parents tremendously. It saddens me to watch the battles they are subjected to everyday. For three years and nine months with the assistance of the Paralyzed Veterans of America service organization, my parents have been battling with the VA and the service for Richard's entitled benefits. The first year after Richard's discharge from the Army, my parents fought with the Department of the Army as a result of the findings of a 'line of duty (LOD)' determination investigation."

An LOD investigation is generally conducted whenever a soldier acquires a disease, incurs a significant injury, or is injured under unusual circumstances. There is a presumption that all diseases, injuries, or deaths occur 'in the line of duty, not as a result of his or her own misconduct.' An LOD investigation helps determine a soldier's entitlement to pay and allowances, accrual of service and leave time, disability, and retirement. A soldier receives these benefits only if the final determination is 'in the line of duty.' Richard was riding his motorcycle off-post within the Army's directives on a Sunday, and required Personal Protective Equipment (PPE). A military member is on duty 24/7, and subject to be called to duty at any minute with limited notification.

During the investigation of the accident, a witness alleged Richard had been drinking beer but was not drunk, which meant it was determined 'not in line of duty, due to own misconduct.' However, there is no available evidence to substantiate the allegation. A record of any blood work to validate that Richard had been drinking has never being found. The investigating officer had determined and reported in his report, Richard was operating the motorcycle recklessly, off-post, under the influence of alcohol, and therefore, found him to be, 'not in line of duty, due to own misconduct.' But in time under a more rigid investigation, the witness admitted to not having seen Richard drinking that day, just that they often had a couple of cold ones together, mostly since returning from Afghanistan. Any time the soldier was not present for duty due to hospitalization, being on quarters, or being on convalescent leave is counted as bad time as a result of the 'not in the line of duty' determination. Bad time has to be made up. Richard was not capable, under the circumstances.

His parents refused to give up fighting their battles. Right after that long fight with the Department of the Army, they were engaged in another type of battle with the Department of Veterans Affairs. Fighting the long waiting game with the unknown, no one returning phone calls or answering the mail in the VA system had been common. "It appeared as if the VA was not accountable or responsible to the public," said Lois. "I just cannot believe it. My son had multiple repeated deployments to Iraq and Afghanistan so these people can enjoy their freedom, only for them to disrespect those who allow them the freedom. It is so wrong, but who holds them accountable? We felt hopeless and helpless trying to care for Richard with his anger and unable not to give much credence to his blame game." It was a final closure to one of the major battles Richard's parents had been fighting. Lois said, "The Paralyzed Veterans of America learned that the main reason Richard's case had been delayed so long was because the VA was unable to locate the conclusive outcome of the 'line of duty' investigation report. Somehow, these reports were nowhere to be found at the National Records Management Center in St. Louis, Missouri, therefore, the case stopped, no one followed up in pursuing another action. Fortunately, the Paralyzed Veterans of America Officer had a copy and was able to provide the Regional Office with a copy for their actions. It was obvious, none of the government systems— the Department of Army, National Records Management Center, Veterans Affairs, and Medical Records community system—had the documents available in their system." Patricia said, "I don't understand how America can put men on the moon, or have the technology for unmanned drones, but are yet unable to arrange government systems which are able to speak to each other. Too many records go into a black hole in the system or there is a wide range of unaccountability." It was evident as I sat across from Patricia and watched the tears run down her face when she said, "I lost both my parents and brother the day of that motorcycle accident. I am also a casualty of that accident and the wars he fought."

Richard finally joined us in the living room, dressed and in his wheelchair, with his parents, where I was seated conversing with Patricia. I formally introduced myself and presented my identification. Richard stared at my badge and asked if I was in the Army or the Marines. When I stated I had been in the Air Force, he laughed and said, "Air Force and Coast Guard are like being in the Girl Scouts." I accepted his humor, and explained, "We all needed each other. I need you and you need me to afford you the best quality of life possible, as it is my honor and privilege as it was in the military. Each branch of the service needs each other to do their job better or complete the required mission." Realizing that we needed a deeper level of trust, I then described how I had done some crazy things on my motorcycle in high school, along with my classmates. I have scars to prove some of the risks I took. This line of conversation was another icebreaker and he started to share some of his stories and was able to answer the questions reasonably. It enabled me to assess his condition and make more informed decisions on what was the best interest of the VA in partnering with him and his family.

Richard's behavior was mirrored by several others who

met the misfortune of being paralyzed. They would often be angry and depressed, questioning why they did not die instead of living like this. Many wish the medic, parents, or first responders had allowed them to die instead of being a parasite or a burden to society. In most cases the victims of such misfortunes are individuals who were very powerful, believed themselves to be invincible, and thought things like this happened only to others, not them. But on the other hand, some people spend all their time trying to enjoy what they have and improve it in any way possible with a vision of being a scientific miracle. That optimism and spirit have allowed progress toward healing and better mental and physical health for many.

Many wounded warriors strive to prove their disabilities are not handicaps, instead an opportunity to move forward in life, and be all they can be. It is amazing how open some veterans would be by saying, "We would give our arms, legs, or sight as gifts for our nation that we might live in freedom," extending their gratitude to the families of the fallen and families of the wounded, for the sacrifices no one can imagine if they have not experienced it. Blaming or feeling sorry for themselves is not an option as a way of life. I have seen veterans with artificial limbs engaged in snow skiing, snowboarding, water skiing, sailing, kayaking, scuba, canoeing, cycling, horseback riding, golf, along with other sports and social activities, giving others hope with great admiration. In particular, I recall a story that was told by a medical person who had met and was a great fan of Christopher Reeve. Perhaps it would be fair to say she was infatuated with the man. She claimed to know Christopher Reeve beyond the world's admiration for him as Superman, and with the accident that dispelled that reality. He was determined, with any resources he could garner, to find a way to heal and help others to recognize their medical condition is not a terminal sentence. He traveled around the country speaking to encourage people that there would be answers in the future and he would do all he could to make that happen. He was driven to do all he could, and gave himself tirelessly to that cause. He believed in hydrotherapy and many other innovative methods, like stem cells and neurotherapy, to improve quality of life. He was a great example of someone who accepts their misfortune as merely a setback and lives life with dignity and courage for the miracle to come.

The agony of the prevailing journey that Richard's family had endured in an effort to obtain his entitled benefits, coupled with the emotional battles his parents had been fighting, were very concerning to me. Having been exposed to both sides of a veteran's behavioral outlook of their medical conditions coupled with the knowledge of the available government agencies and services to partner with the parents, I had a compelling need to share these options with the family. Knowing the body of work the local Wounded Warriors offer, the devoted high level of caring services the social worker team at the VA Medical Center provides to the community could be a wonderful turning point in their lives. I was not sure if Richard's behavior or words of hating government agencies were to the same depth as some of those true anti-government veterans I have visited. But I knew for sure, having visited with several traumatic brain injury (TBI) veterans and witnessing the outcome of their therapy with the partnership of the local Wounded Warriors program, and the VA Social Worker Out-Base Team program, Richard would be in good hands. His parents had been fighting to get to this point with the assistance of the Paralyzed Veterans of

America, and were deeply emotional to see the light at the end of the tunnel. They stated, "We are especially grateful Richard did not act up any worse to delay this remarkable end. We hope you will visit with us again because we are sure Richard does not want to be placed in a psych ward." It was obvious to everyone those were the words to best manage Richard's behavior.

The apparent change in his attitude allowed me to realize that Richard's question of: "Why couldn't I have died instead of living like this?" would be answered and appreciated with professional assistance and the partnership of the local Wounded Warriors program, and the VA Social Worker Out-Base Team program. I made it clear, I was not a healthcare professional, but a reasonable person, who believes that Richard could be a positive example for others to emulate.

I also explained that I believe Richard may now acknowledge he was protected during his multiple repeated deployments to Iraq and Afghanistan by some type of higher power and now can make a difference. Based on his comment, "the Air Force and Coast Guard are like being in the Girl Scouts," I realized duty, pride, and commitment were very important to him. Coupled with his tours in the war zone, he would relish the opportunity to show, "I can do it," just as those TBI veterans and athletes do.

The family was provided contact information as an opportunity to partner with others in affording Richard with the best quality of life possible. Patricia said, "Your visit today has been that miracle I have prayed would come to assist my parents and change my brother's focus on life."

CHAPTER FIVE

The Difficult Pilgrimage of the Traumatic Brain Injury Spouse

"The young patriots now returning from war in Iraq
and Afghanistan and other deployments worldwide are
joining the ranks of veterans to whom America owes
an immense debt of gratitude."

– FORMER U.S. REPRESENTATIVE STEVE BUYER

The actuality of visiting the polytrauma unit at the Tampa VA Medical Center for the first time and witnessing a nineteen-year-old soldier hooked up to all kinds of medical equipment with tubes, wires, and bags of medications going into his body, is a shocking testament of the harsh struggle the family endures and the price our society pays for world freedom. It was truly a moment of awareness into the seriousness of the disabilities that our wounded warriors with traumatic brain injury (TBI) experience.

It all began while I was meeting another veteran, and suddenly, my cell phone rang. The strange thing about this moment is the fact I rarely take my cell phone into an interview or meeting, and to have it on was inexplicable. The nursing home administrator, business office manager, nurse manager, the veteran's spouse Tanya, and I were sitting around the administrator's conference room table. We were doing our best to defuse a sensitive, embarrassing moment. The certified nursing assistant (CNA) mistakenly addressed and introduced the veteran's spouse as a caretaker. The spouse, Tanya, got very angry, loud, and accused the CNA of being disrespectful, with racial intent. The veteran was a Caucasian schizophrenic patient with post-traumatic stress disorder (PTSD), and the spouse, an African American. The CNA assumed for some reason this lady was the veteran's caretaker. Ironically, Tanya had arrived at the nursing home with a male companion and introduced him as her cousin.

During the time I had to step out to take the urgent phone call, the nurse manager and Tanya's companion went out of the conference room for a cup of coffee. The nurse manager asked him if he wanted a cup for his cousin Tanya. He made it clear, "Tanya is not my cousin, and as a matter of fact she is my spouse." A few minutes later, I walked back into the room, apologized for leaving the meeting and explained how my supervisor was directed to summon me to drop everything I was doing, and go to the Tampa VA Medical Center Polytrauma Unit immediately. It was to visit an Operation Iraqi Freedom and Operation Enduring Freedom (OIF/OEF) Conflicts veteran who had experienced traumatic brain injuries. The Regional Office had received an inquiry from a congressman on this veteran. As directed, I cancelled the meeting and rescheduled it for another day. Cancellation of the meeting only angered Tanya more. She accused me of being insensitive to what she believed to have been racist behavior of the nursing home staff and that I had cancelled the meeting to run away from the issue. It was interesting to me because Tanya and I have had several telephone conversations concerning a face-to-face meeting with her and the requirement for information on her to be a fiduciary spouse payee. She was somewhat apprehensive with the face-to-face meeting between the veteran, herself, and me. When we first met in the lobby at the nursing home, to her dismay I was also black. She said, "You don't look like the Miguel I was expecting." I explained, "It happens often and I had nothing to do with choosing my name. Let us blame my mother for that." I reminded her of our earlier meeting in the lobby, the error in her perception, and our conversation. I made it clear it was not my intent to minimize or justify the root cause of the CNA's behavior. I would leave the final action on what is best, up to the nursing home management staff. It was my expectation she would understand and appreciate my predicament of not being in the business of legislating racial awareness practices.

I continued to clarify the urgency of the call I had received, with its clear instructions to, "drop whatever I was doing and go visit a patient in the Tampa VA Medical Center." I agreed to reschedule the meeting whenever it was convenient for Tanya. She requested to meet the following Saturday at 9:00 a.m. on her day off, and I accepted. The nurse manager escorted me to my vehicle and expressed her concern about the information Tanya's companion shared with her when I left the room. I assured her I would investigate the allegations and take the necessary actions as a potential abuse of benefits and misuse of funds, if the facts were proven to be such.

Rescheduling the appointment with Tanya garnered me an opportunity to conduct a quality investigation on the veteran's marital status. The day following my visit, a VA social worker from the home health team visited the veteran. The facility staff informed her of the chain of events with Tanya the previous day, in regards to her divorcing the veteran, but receiving his benefits. The VA social worker had expressed the seriousness of these allegations and formally requested a fiduciary field examiner investigation, which I later conducted. The nursing home business office manager had gone into the public records of Tanya, only to discover some shocking information, requiring immediate action. The documents showed Tanya had divorced the veteran March 1, three years prior, and married her so-called cousin September 27, the following year. The veteran had adopted Tanya's son ten years prior. The veteran is 100 percent permanently and totally disabled, which authorizes his spouse to receive paid educational benefits. It was a bucket of snakes and I had to compile all the evidence to support what I had believed to be a fraudulent case. The Saturday morning meeting was very short. Tanya attempted to cover up her guilt with an outburst of anger, accusation of invasion of privacy, racism, and threats. I said, "Tanya, facts don't lie, people lie about facts, and the evidence I provided supports these facts as I know them to be. You will get your day in court to appeal the evidence we were able to obtain from the public record as facts." She walked out of the meeting. I immediately had the veteran's benefits suspended, pending the decision on the allegations. A letter was drafted with the attached evidence and an explanation for my supervisor, management, and the inspector general or general counsel's review.

Upon my arrival at the Tampa VA Medical Center I was

provided the documents the Regional Office had e-mailed there, to conduct the field examination. The VA Regional Office public contact representative had received the e-mail with instructions for me. The urgency of this case was clear in the instructions provided. Since it was the first time visiting such specialized staff in the polytrauma unit, I had to employ my healthcare professional training. The unit is a mixture of amazing state-of-the art science, deep concerns for the political intent, and the staff being over-protective of patient confidentiality. The perception I had, was the staff's lack of trust outside the VA medical community. As usual, I identified myself as a VA employee from the Regional Office, in the benefits department, before meeting with the staff, the veteran, and his spouse. The medical team briefing was to the point and clear as they explained: "The OIF/OEF conflicts have resulted in an increased number of veterans who have experienced traumatic brain injuries (TBI) during their tour of service. The Veterans' Brain Injury Center estimates that approximately 22 percent of all combat casualties from these conflicts are brain injuries, compared to a rate of 12 percent for Vietnam War veterans. 60 to 80 percent of soldiers who have other blast injuries may also have TBI. The VA has initiated the polytrauma system of care, which treats veterans with TBI who have also experienced musculoskeletal, neurological, and psychological trauma and we want to ultimately provide better outcomes for the thousands of men and women serving our country on the front lines, and not be a part of the politics. Our patients and their families are a vital part of the rehabilitation treatment team. They are involved with goal-setting and meeting with team members to develop a plan of care and set goals for guiding our patients in reaching their maximum level of independence."

In an effort to garner their trust and perhaps appreciate my level of understanding of the predicament we were facing, I presented the fact that I am an Air Force retired veteran who had served as a healthcare administrator, in the medical community for more than eighteen of my thirty years of active duty. It was clear, the veteran and his family's best interests are first and foremost over politics, but the facts are, I am here because I was directed by a politician to investigate this matter and we all have a moral, ethical, and legal obligation to serve and care for the veteran. I have disregarded any personal feelings I may have with an expectation of being objective, and employed a reasonable person approach to the facts. This was based on the literature I had glanced over recently, which spoke to TBI being the signature injury of the current wars in Iraq and Afghanistan. Military doctors and leaders in the field are educated in TBI and know that early screening is critical to diagnose and treat the disease from mild to severe cases. I was well aware as in ages past, wounded warriors were always well cared for as a result of their sacrifice, with dedication and efforts to afford them the best quality of life. There would be "no one left behind." Today's VA cutting-edge programs for wounded warriors in all areas of healthcare from amputations and traumatic brain injuries to psychological damage, including rehab programs, to name a few, are next to none. The healthcare professionals are well trained and equipped to handle the most comprehensive care. They partner with leading universities and medical professionals with world-renowned, state-of-the-art medical science. They are encouraged and feel profound gratitude from great outcomes for the opportunities to provide this cutting-edge care.

I was neither mentally nor emotionally prepared to

experience the real casualties of today's war. After the intense meeting with the medical treatment team and walking into the private room down the hall for a face-to-face visit with the veteran Shannon and his spouse Allison, I was astonished. The sight of a nineteen-year-old U.S. Army Afghanistan veteran, who was connected and surrounded with all kinds of state-of-the-art life-support machines, was a life-changing experience for me. There sat his spouse at the bedside stroking his arm, choking back tears, struggling with all kinds of emotions, yet gracefully welcoming me into the room.

This atrocity of war, coupled with the struggles of caring for their fifteen-month-old son, and fighting her mother-in-law and her attorneys for spousal rights over her perceived entitled rights had been totally unknown to me then. The need was for Allison to live life now with new meaning and purpose, through the looming unknown was clear. I realized the veteran's severe medical conditions had in addition some other serious issues when Allison said, "Everything about this visit and meeting with you was arranged by Mrs. McKenzie's attorneys through the courts. The amount of time I spend with Shannon, how much money I am allowed each day, and his mother's controlling ways have been a way of life. The McKenzie family and I will not visit Shannon at the same time. This is his mother's wish. I could not be happier to see you. Our county service officer and the Disabled American Veterans representatives told me, the field examiner would accumulate facts, investigate the validity, and do what is in the best interest of the veteran and his dependents. The county service officers and Disabled American Veterans have been my God-sent lifeline, the best, kind-hearted, and knowledgeable group of people available during these trying times. Each one of them had nothing but good things to say about the field examiner in Tampa. I only want to be taken care of and continue sharing all the love the Lord gave me with my family, as I transform these sorrows into happiness and joy. How do I live life with new meaning, to continue loving the new person I am married to along with his mother's drama?" She continued fighting back those tears, apologized for being emotional, and said, "The biggest loser is our son and Mrs. McKenzie is too stubborn to realize it."

The unconditional sacrifices, devotion, commitments, unlimited price, and sorrows the families of the service members endure for the world's freedom were evident in this veteran's room. The sight of this young Army veteran with the right side of his face scarred and badly deformed as a result of the loss of inner and outer cranial damage, was only a glimpse of other medical conditions beyond the human eyes. The skin grafts throughout the right upper extremity with residuals of a craniotomy, along with the white band around his neck and a porthole for a tracheal tube to assist with breathing were obvious. Allison said, "Ever since that dreadful day in September 2010 when Shannon suffered severe burns and traumatic brain injuries, then later losing part of his skull, use of his right hand and foot, developing kidney calcification, and lumbar scoliosis with several other medical conditions from a roadside explosion in Afghanistan, my life has been a never-ending nightmare. It has been a bad dream that will never end and I just want to wake up. It appears as if Mrs. McKenzie's attacks have worsened in an effort to deflect her deep sadness. The borderline insanity of her behavior was incomprehensible to me. The courts and her attorneys are trying to live our lives at a time when unity is in the best interest of everyone.

"Being a hairdresser was not good enough for the

McKenzie's son. It was even said, "What can an uneducated hair dresser from the housing projects bring to the McKenzies as representative in the community?" Mrs. McKenzie is a registered nurse and her spouse an accountant. Shannon's older sister and I were high school classmates and best friends until her mother found out Shannon had been interested in me. Shannon's sister, Beverly, went on to the university and became a board-certified physician's assistant. I was a cashier at our local bowling alley. Shannon was sixteen and I nineteen with a vehicle. I use to give him a ride home after closing. We became best friends and confidants. One thing leads to another after eighteen months of being friends. He would always make it clear, "I was his best friend and soul mate." We were able talk about everything or anything that was going on in our world. Our friendship angered his mother. It was no secret his mother was a very controlling, take-charge woman.

"During the early part of the pregnancy, Mrs. McKenzie claimed the baby was not Shannon's and accused me of entrapment and statutory rape. It truly angered Shannon and he had a problem getting over his mother's nasty ways. The harder she fought, the more stubborn he was toward everything she advocated. Two weeks after his graduation from high school we were married, and he enlisted into the U.S. Army as an Airborne Ranger in defiance of his mother's controlling ways. His immediate plans were to have the Army pay for his higher education. He claimed, 'it was the best thing for us all.' His mother's all-out attacks were furious. She had a paternity test of our son conducted, which proved Shannon was the father. He never forgave her for publicly embarrassing him, by showing the lack of trust and being disrespectful. It saddens me to no end because I always admired her as a very strong woman. I never expected to be disrespected and have to endure the constant harassment. It was amazing to see Mr. McKenzie's congeniality, right after the DNA test was completed declaring, 'It is more likely than not, Shannon is the father.' He was very vocal in accepting his grandson with such pride, as the child will carry on his family's name. Mr. McKenzie became the voice of reason for my family, which has minimized the battles, insults, and struggles with Mrs. McKenzie. I always told her, 'I may not be well-educated, but I'm wise with the knowledge from the school of hard knocks, as a hairdresser, and we need to work together in the best interest of both Shannon and the baby.'"

Allison expressed her gratitude to the senator of South Carolina, who is a highly respected, influential, active member of the Armed Forces Committee. She said, "If it was not for one of my customers' persistence on me contacting the senator's office for assistance, Shannon's mother and her high-powered attorneys would have taken over everything I may be entitled to. The senator is known for asking the hard questions and taking the Armed Forces and the Department of Veterans Affairs to task. Therefore the VA did not provide me with the old window dressing and standard answer, 'We have received your application for benefits. It is our sincere desire to decide your case promptly. However, as we have a great number of claims, action on your case may be delayed. We are still processing your application for compensation. We apologize for the delay. You will be notified upon completion of processing.'"

The Disabled American Veterans representative showed me a ton of such letters received on other veterans' files. The number of pending cases has increased in the last eight years. There was no mention of the increased number of newly hired government employees within this same period of time, with no change in the service to veterans and their dependents. I was told it has been an increase of over 200 percent in hiring within the fiduciary unit and a large night crew added in the Regional Office. Yet, beneficiaries are still dying in large numbers before their claims are processed and unable to receive their entitled benefits with the 200 percent staff increase. Something is wrong with this picture!

A couple of days after I had completed a thorough investigation, reviewing the fiduciary guidelines criteria to appoint the spouse as a spouse payee and appointing Allison, spouse payee, I received a phone call from Mrs. McKenzie's attorney. He expressed his concerns and disappointment with our position in appointing Allison as the fiduciary spouse payee for the veteran. His first words were, "You don't know that lady, and it is because of her, Mr. McKenzie ran away from home, got married, enlisted into the military, and now his life is on a balance. She is not financially astute to manage their funds reasonably. The courts in our state have granted his mother power of attorney and she should, without question, be appointed fiduciary payee for her son." I begged the difference of the attorney immediately. I said, "I may not know Allison to the extent you believe to know her but I question how well you know me, for you to make such a profound statement of my character and knowledge." I also questioned his knowledge of the VA Statutory Laws and the standard operating procedures the government employs in appointing a fiduciary spouse payee. I expressed my appreciation with him for sharing the court's position of appointing Mrs. McKenzie as an attorney-in-fact for her son. I made it clear: The VA recognizes every court-appointed guardianship, but a power of attorney is a state document the VA does not accept. The government reserves the rights to appoint a fiduciary payee in the best interests of the veteran. Allison met both the guidelines and the thorough background review, without disqualifying criteria. I explained, "The VA does not find the mother's appointment as attorney-in-fact to be qualified or disqualified. The veteran's wishes are not in question as a result of his state of being and circumstance. Enabling a potentially complete stranger to control his VA funds is not a recognizable issue." I requested his assistance if he had any facts contrary to the evidence on file to please forward them to the Regional Office for our review and actions. It is noted the only person who profits from guardianships are attorneys in most cases when there is no proven potential reason for abuse or misuse of funds.

Allison said, "Mrs. McKenzie realized everyone will not dance to her drumbeat, but it was not about looking good, but doing the right things right. I believe Mr. McKenzie's reasonable approach and not blaming is better for the future of their son or grandson. Therefore, she could not legally control our lives and be a part of her grandson's life without my consent. I was Shannon's legal spouse, fiduciary spouse payee, and the mother of his son. My respect and admiration for her had never wavered, despite the perceived borderline insanity of her behavior. Because I strongly believe, 'Love is patient, love is kind, it does not envy, it does not boast, it not proud, it is not rude, it not self-seeking, it is not easily angered, it keeps no records of wrong or right.' I love Shannon and our son, and with God's interventions I will stand next to them both against any man. I have nothing but time sitting here reflecting on so many shared words. The stories and dreams of doors opening for Shannon with an education without his parents' assistance were nothing but an unrealistic fantasy. Our expectations of life and the type of father he would be with his children seem to be impossible. I constantly hear our conversation and share the guilt of not being able to convince him not to enlist into the U.S. Army as an Airborne Ranger to fight, but instead to serve in a job that would allow him to learn a trade. He wanted to be the best-of-the-best and he believed the Airborne Rangers were that and more. It was not safe nor in the best interest of the family. He also wanted to be an honorable man, give me his name, and give his child a name without the label of an illegitimate child. Shannon strongly believed being married would alleviate his mother's notions of filing a case of statutory rape because of our age difference."

Allison said, "The guilt and blame is such a battle that totally consumes me, minute by minute every day, and I don't know how to shake it as I sit in the room with Shannon not knowing for sure what is next with Mrs. McKenzie. I have to be strong for the sake of Shannon, Junior, and pray the McKenzie family will be the support system we need to have the best life possible. I am not sure who will be covering our son's and my medical expenses now we no longer have the military Tricare system available to us. He is no longer on active duty and those entitlements do not apply in the veteran system. The insecurity and the unknown of life after the military is one of my greatest fears." I shared my deep appreciation and respect for the VA healthcare system and services as a holistic entity. I also explained how I would confer with the VA Health Care Eligibility Department to ensure she was provided clear, detailed information on access to care in the VA medical community. It was obvious to me Allison was also a war casualty and needed medical assistance herself. Therefore, I contacted the social worker team at the Tampa VA Medical Center, ascertained information on all the VA health benefits, to include the CHAMPVA and Wounded Warriors' support programs and services with contacts and phone numbers.

CHAPTER SIX

The Kent State University Shooting Haunts Him

"Our nation must provide sufficient access to healthcare,
adequate benefits, and the supplemental resources
our veterans were promised and so dearly need.
We owe our heroes no less."

– U. S. Representative Dan Lipinski

Edward hears voices no one else hears and sees the faces of those students at Kent State University that no one else sees. They are the memories of his time with the Ohio State Army National Guard, fulfilling his military service obligation following a tour in the Republic of Vietnam as a trained U.S. Marine. He tried to survive each day after serving in the jungles of Vietnam and then witnessed a traumatic event of this nation that was labeled "a murder mystery."

From my view, establishing mutual trust for an information-sharing environment can be a mind-boggling experience with someone who has such deep issues. It was difficult—as I was sitting on the other side of the veteran's dining room table, looking into his piercing blue eyes, and watching his body language—to try to understand or to appreciate how we can make this work. I was stunned to hear him say, "The middle child of most families would often blame their position as the reason for having to prove themselves over everyone and everything within the family or in life." Edward readily believes it is the root cause for his rocky pilgrimage in life. To try twice as hard and get half as far is an acceptable way of life in his world.

Edward was the second child with an older brother he unconditionally admired and respected. He said, "My brother was very good at whatever he did. Our mother's favored child and her lifeline." There was no doubt his mother loved his brother more than life. His younger sister, whom he described as someone with external beauty and internal brains, turned out to be a research medical scientist and his father's heartstring. Most people believed his father only had one child from the way he talked about her to everyone. The middle child, Edward, was born in Flatbush, in Brooklyn, New York, and along with his brother, moved to Ohio with their parents at a very young age. They were west of the Pennsylvania state line in an area known as "the steel valley" during the glory days, with much of the industrial economy that drew various opportunities for employment.

His mother, an accountant, was a very strong-willed woman. She was well respected in the community for her ability to get the job done. Edward said that his mother wore the pants in their family and his dad accepted his role. For some reason his father had a hard time holding down a job. He was a law school graduate, but was unable to pass the bar exam and found getting employment as an attorney somewhat difficult. Growing up, one of Edward's philosophies was, "Life is like a garden, and I will dig it." It was okay not to have any great ambitions to be anything special in life. He went through school as an average student, not applying himself. He smoked some weed, drank beer, and worked on his friends' cars as something to do. That was the way he described his school days.

After graduating from high school, Edward and one of his drinking buddies were hired as electrical engineer apprentices, making good money for kids without ambition or a desire to go to college. "It was too good to be real," said Edward, in regards to this opportunity. "Mother gave me an ultimatum, go to school or get a job." He claimed this is why the opportunity meant so much to him. The look on his face spoke volumes of his pride. It turned out his boss, Mr. Jones, was an old business friend of his mother. Neither Edward nor Mr. Jones knew of each other. Mr. Jones was not even aware of Edward's mother having a second son. This is when Edward made it clear why his brother was well known in their family. His brother was the high school football quarterback who led the team to the district championship. He was also the class leader and voted by his classmates as most likely to succeed. It was amazing to what extent Edward went, to justify why things in his life were the way they were for a middle child.

In December 1967 he received the infamous "Greetings from the President of the United States" to report for induction—the draft notice. Edward said this was very disappointing and the beginning of his depression. He had finally found a purpose, being an electrical engineer apprentice with a preceptor who cared about him. The thought of that day still angers him. It was too late to volunteer for the Air Force, Navy, or Coast Guard as a means of reducing the chances of being exposed to combat. Many draftees had fled the country, but the fear of not being financially capable of supporting himself in another country—and the unknown—deterred him from being a draft dodger. He explained he not only did not have the necessary finances, neither did he have an educational background, nor the skills to offer society. His mother would never support that lifestyle. He did not pursue the educational journey his mother suggested nor did he have any interest in religious training as a means of deferment. Therefore, he reported as instructed in the draft notice early that morning to the induction center. It was a very short night after drinking with a couple of friends and being concerned with where the Army would send him after basic training. Little did Edward know the Army had no followed-on assignment for him after basic training, because the Marines drafted him. Edward's recollection of this day was, "It was one of the coldest days in Ohio. I showed up with a big hangover from the night before, with little sleep, and late, because the weather was so bad and the bus was off schedule. The sergeant told me it was okay because some members of his staff were also late and to take a seat in the big ceremony room with some other recruits. A couple of hours later, members from each branch of the services came into the room and called out the names of the members for their service. Draftees' names were called by the U.S. Army sergeant, and we were told to stand against the perimeter of the room with our belongings. Then we were told to count from one to five, but the guy next to me, who also had a bad hangover from drinking the night before, slipped off to the men's room. Therefore, I was number five and every fifth person was drafted into the Marines. I was not mentally, emotionally, or physically prepared to be a Marine. I called my mother to explain what had happened. She claimed it was not legal and she made some phone calls, but to no avail. I was on an airplane to Parris Island, South Carolina, for 121 days of U.S. Marine Corps boot champ as a draftee with two years' active duty commitment. I was informed there was an increased need for manpower, congressional authorization, and I was drafted into the Marines.

"I had been drinking water, chewing gum, and sucking peppermint candy to cover up my hangover from the night before. We got off the bus and the drill instructor saw me chewing gum. He said, 'Boy! What are you eating?' I said 'Nothing,' as I turned and spat the gum on the ground. This man got up into my face, the brim of his cap was on my nose and he went crazy. He started screaming, 'Pick it up off my ground,' with a big push with his foot on my back towards the ground. I naturally bent over and picked the gum up off the ground. This man got crazier than before, screaming at the top of his lungs as he questioned the way the gum got on the ground. He said it was from my mouth and I needed to pick it up the same way, with my mouth. I got down on all fours with his foot on my back, picked the gum up with my teeth, and swallowed it. The drill instructor informed us all, 'the first word out of your mouth is, "Sir" and the last word is "Sir," I am your mother and your daddy and no one eats, drinks, sleeps, or goes to my bathrooms unless you are told to do so by a drill instructor. You will not eat or drink unless we give it to you, you will not wear or use anything unless it is issued to you. If we did not issue it to you, it does not belong to you, which includes watches, rings, chains, or medications. Am I clear? Am I clear?' Everyone said, 'Sir, yes Sir.' He said, 'You will give your soul to God because your ass belongs to me.' Everyone answered again, 'Sir, yes Sir,' at the top of their lungs. It was about 12:45 a.m. and our day had just started at Parris Island. We had to stand on some yellow footprints for alignment information, for processing at the reception station. I thought it was the longest day of my life, with only having had two or three hours' sleep and a hangover the day before. Then no sleep the first days at Parris Island. The next morning at 0500 hours a 5'6", 160-lb. sergeant walked into the open bay barracks screaming to get up, banging trashcan covers, and throwing people out of beds. It was truly a rude awakening.

"He was a little person with a big attitude who suffered from a little person's syndrome. This was the first person I ever hated and would love to meet again in a back alley. He told us to be out front in ten minutes. It was very hard for forty-five men to go to the bathroom, which was totally open, arms-length away from each other, in view of each other while others were showering. The sand fleas were described by the drill instructor as sacred and forbidden. The drill instructor said, 'If it ever comes to our attention some dumb ass ever caused harm to one of these sacred pets, just give your soul to God, because your ass belongs to me.'" The look on Edward's face as he retold that moment in his life was priceless.

The tone of his voice in the explanation of the most memorable thing about boot camp is totally worth telling again. Edward said the way everyone's hair was cut, breaking the recruits down, being divested of ego, morals, or any personal issues, then molding them into men of character with lots of courage, the Marine way, was like a bad dream and hard to endure for someone who only wanted to get by. He also told the story of the day he was going on a ten-mile march and his feet were killing him. He told the drill instructor and the instructor told him, "Marines don't feel pain; pain is only a distraction to a successful ending."

"The Marine Corps Boot Camp was mentally, physically, and emotionally tasking with the great threat of being recycled back to the first week, which made the impossible, possible. This threat kept us all focused on moving forward and overcoming every obstacle," said Edward. "In my world prior to basic training, water was necessary for drinking or washing only, not playing or swimming in. In my case, playing in the water was my great fear, but the squad leader worked with me in the water and I worked with him on classroom matters such as U.S. Marine Corps history, starting with the ranks, drill and ceremony, or how best to remember *The Marines' Hymn*. It was also amazing to watch those overweight recruits on their special diet come down to standard and the underweight buff up to standard. Most of us cooperated and most graduated. The countless hours spent with our best friend—the M16 Rifle—was beyond crazy. The hours spent on the characteristics of the M16, taking the rifle apart, cleaning it thoroughly, and putting it back together was something every recruit could do in their sleep." But the continuous training he received on the M16 was greatly appreciated on the ground during his tour in Vietnam. Out of nowhere Edward said, "I needed the discipline, a purpose in life, instead of feeling sorry for myself or constantly expecting the worst. Some self-direction was lacking and the self-confidence instilled in me by the Marine Corps was something I did not know existed. I found the means of inner peace, instead of the nagging thoughts of blaming being the middle child when things do not go my way."

Edward was a little emotional as he shared the story of the moment when the chief drill instructor, Staff Sergeant Steve, offered him a recommendation for meritorious promotion upon graduation from basic training, stating, "The platoon in general appreciated how you found time to assist them all with the classroom academics and encourage them through the basic training journey. No one knew how you found the time to do the things you were able to do for them, or why you did what you had done for the platoon, so the U.S. Marine Corps appreciates your leadership talents." He was more emotional as he said, "I was a nobody from Ohio, with a little of my mother's DNA and intellectual skills and used it as a way to distract myself and survive the nightmare of boot camp. I got promoted to Private First Class (PFC) with the Leatherneck Dress Blues. Believe me, to be somebody who is respected and accepted by the U.S. Marine Corps at Parris Island is truly an honor and for me to be honored by Staff Sergeant Steve, was totally unreal." Edward wanted to be clear about his experience as he said, "Boot camp was not a walk in the park by any stretch of your imagination for this non-jock kid whose only exercise was beer curls with my drinking friends. It was very hard, but finding mental distraction to overcome those fears and obstacles throughout the journey could be interpreted as mind over matter. I was not a gung-ho person, just humble enough to know I had the smarts to be accepted and respected. The drill instructor also informed 22 of the 40 graduating Marines from our platoon of the requirement for us to attend the 22-day battle skills training after the Military Occupation Specialties (MOS) training before going to Vietnam."

Going to Vietnam after completing 121 days of basic training, coupled with the 22 days of battle skills training, and watching Audie Murphy in old war movies with his dad on TV as a child gave him the false sense of invincibility. The tour in Vietnam started off on the wrong foot, Edward said.

During the in-processing at the reception station in Da Nang, he and a couple of his drinking buddies contracted venereal disease as they recklessly had sex along the way with some working girls. Therefore, the three of them had to spend two extra weeks at the reception station in Da Nang for medical care including daily penicillin shots, which required monitoring for possible side effects. This was "A-Okay" for them because somehow he got his hands on some real good weed, marijuana laced with opium, for those hard days in the jungle. He said, those two weeks in garrison were nothing but one high after another and he remembers crying for the first two days after processing, watching casualties arriving, Marine after Marine. So when the Mama-san—Vietnamese female hooch keeper—got him some weed, everything in his life was perfect. It prepared him to see things much better, later in the field. It was all in slow motion, he claimed. The Marines had suffered heavy casualties at Khe Sanh, but it was under control. The road to Khe Sanh (Route 9) was open. The talk was, that was the campaign that got General West-moreland replaced in June 1968. The media displayed lack of confidence in his leadership abilities.

The 1st Corps area in Dang Ha, the most-forward area in the DMZ, Alpha 3 area, had suffered a higher amount of casualties and being a Machine Gunner-0331, that's where Edward's skills were greatly needed. Edward said, "With the best weed in the world, the training I had received, and those old Audie Murphy movies, I just could not wait to get into action." Two days later, at the age of 19, the Viet Cong were shooting at him and he was shooting at them until they were dead. With a weapon that shot 500 bullets a minute he felt invincible. His fellow Marines called him the Neutralizer. But throughout our conversation, Edward constantly gave credit to God or his guardian angel that covered him with the blood of Jesus, because the life expectancy of a Machine Gunner-0331 in Vietnam was a couple of minutes, since Charlie's—the Viet Cong's—main objective is to take out the machine gunner. The North Vietnamese Army had occupied Hill 881, a great strategic post, and the brass decided the Marines needed it and paid very heavily for that strategic position. Edward's machine gun was needed to preserve it. His drill instructor at the battle skill training had fought on this hill and told them about the bunkers and everything about the hill he was protecting. He sat on the ridge of the hill with his weed and machine gun, enjoying the view when the fog would lift to allow him to see the beauty of the countryside. He stood guard, ensuring neither the Viet Cong nor the North Vietnamese army troops would take this beauty back. On October 16, 1968, Edward's platoon was ambushed and he and several other Marines were injured in a firefight with ten deaths.

Edward was medevaced to the Cam Ranh Bay air base hospital for care and later rehabilitation of his wounds, ready for duty in January 1969. He then returned to duty on the front line again because his machine gun skills were needed. Unlike most wounded warriors, Edward was kept in the war zone for rehabilitation. He explained how the need for a machine gunner in the jungles of Vietnam was vital to any unit. It was expected for him to do the things he was trained to do best with an inexplicable guardian angel looking over him each day until his tour of duty was completed in Vietnam.

Edward was discharged from the Marine Corps at the port, which was an early out of his enlistment contract, having less than 90 days remaining on his contract. Upon his return to the United States, he had an expectation to resume his life in Ohio as a new, confident, self-assured, respectable man who believed he was not just the middle child with nothing to offer society. He had masked his demons with the Marine Corps-imposed self-confidence.

Edward, as with most Vietnam veterans, was ashamed to have served in the Republic of Vietnam during that time in his life. He still had more than four years of service remaining on his obligatory military contract. As a means of reducing the chances of going back into combat, he enlisted into the Ohio Army National Guard to fulfill this obligation. Watching television, listening to the news, and seeing what the world had to say about the war only angered Edward, because he knew precisely what was going on in that part of the world and why—survival. It was only because we were ordered to control communism and that is what we did best, following orders as American fighting men. Edward claimed to have read an article from the *Wall Street Journal* about a Vietnamese official who accepted the unconditional surrender of South Vietnam in 1975. He alleged the official said, "The Americans were fighting on two fronts, the Vietnam battlefield and back at home in America through the antiwar movement on college campuses and in the media."

The Vietnamese leadership listened to and manipulated the American evening news: Jane Fonda visited Hanoi and was photographed seated on an anti-aircraft battery. After two weeks of visiting young soldiers, she said they were not our enemies. What did she know? She was filmed singing a song called "Day Ma Di" written by an anti-war South Vietnamese student. She even made ten radio broadcasts denouncing American political and military leadership as "war criminals." Then the former Attorney General Ramsey

Clark visited and reported on U.S. war crimes in Indochina. These issues gave their leadership confidence they could continue on their battlefield for victory. They may, "lose the battles but win the war." Edward said, "America lost because of its democracy; through dissent and the protests, it lost the ability to mobilize a will to win." I took offense to that statement because I know from personal experience the troops on the front lines never lost their will to win.

Adjusting to the National Guard way of life was quite a culture shock for a Marine Corps-trained, Vietnam veteran during the monthly drill weeks. Edward was able to return to his old job, an electrical engineer apprentice. He completed the program a couple of years later. His mentor, Mr. Jones, had somewhat adopted him like a son, always commending him for his military sense of responsibility and self-respect. Mr. Jones also assisted him with his independence, obtaining a home after moving out of his parents' home. His first spouse for 18 years, and the mother of his only child Mary, was Mr. Jones' niece Lillian. Edward recalled her as his lifeline, his soul mate, and best friend.

Lillian took the infamous call for him to report for duty about 1800 hours, when Mayor LeRoy Satrom declared a state of emergency on May 2, 1970, and Governor Jim Rhodes ordered the Ohio Army National Guard to report for duty to control the crowd at Kent State. It is understood the role of the state National Guard is to assist civilian authorities in maintaining order in extraordinary circumstances. Edward claimed to have remembered the enlistment oath he took, "swore to support the constitution of the United States of America against all enemies, foreign or domestic." These students were not enemies; they were confused about what we were doing in Vietnam. We were only keeping the wars off our shores and controlling the domino effect of communism. He could not help but remember the My Lai massacre of unarmed civilians, mostly children and women, in Vietnam. He also remembered being a Marine in Vietnam fighting to stay alive and yet, "Here I am being asked to defend myself from some kids who were angry because they had the freedom of being free." Edward was very deep for a veteran who was deemed incompetent for VA purposes. For some reason he trusted me and needed to share the reason why he heard those voices and saw those faces. He said, "Any reasonable person would understand, if they had my journey, and seen death as I had seen it." Edward went on to say, "This is what I see or hear almost daily. I hear the voices of the students screaming, the cheering of the students while the Reserve Officer Training Corps (ROTC) building burned and what they perceived to be a successful connection of a rock on a Kent fireman or police officer. I hear obscenities, the sound of the fired tear gas, and each and every shot fired on May 4, 1970, as if I was in Vietnam during a firefight. I see the students cutting the firemen's hoses, preventing them from putting the fire out, the rocks being thrown at the Guardsmen. I saw the aftermath of each and every one of those bullets fired at the students, but who shot them has been a mystery to me and has haunted me ever since. I see the faces of those kids that were shot, much like the 33 killed during my first firefight in the DMZ at Dang Ha. I still don't know who gave the order to fire or can't even remember hearing the order to shoot and don't know who shot those bullets. These thoughts and a clear vision of each of these events haunt me just about every day. Some days are worse than others. It was the straw that broke the camel's back. I requested a discharge for medical reasons from the National Guard, which was granted, and

I had a very hard life after that."

Edward said, "Thanks to Lillian, I did not drink myself to death. I tried drowning those haunting memories or tried to find the best weed in the world like I had in Vietnam. Then my brother Bernard had a massive heart attack and died, which meant my dear mother died as well, despite the fact he was survived by a spouse and two children." The sudden death of his brother, coupled with the shame of being a part the Army National Guard and a Vietnam veteran only sent Edward deeper into a massive depression. His spouse Lillian sought assistance in having Edward admitted to the mental ward. Edward claimed not to understand why the good Lord had to take his brother who had more to offer society than he and with the voices nagging him daily, keeping a gainful employment was not possible. In between all those dreadful moments in his life, Lillian was diagnosed with breast cancer and five years later, she died of ovarian cancer.

The thoughts and memories of those dreadful days at Kent State, the guilt or inability to comprehend why he did not die in Vietnam, while all those great Marines around him did, daily consumed Edward. He said, "I hated God for taking my wonderful brother and leaving me. I had finally hit bottom, believing life was not worth it, I had done something wrong in life or just because I was this middle child I was given a bad hand and did not want it. I met this retired Marine gunnery sergeant who reminded me, 'Being sorry for yourself is like pain, it is only a distraction to a great end, and I needed to get up off my ass and be a man.'" He was disappointed with the VA system, which would allow such a medically troubled, disabled veteran with terrible service-connected conditions to not receive his entitled benefits. Edward said, "The gunnery sergeant asked me, 'How could this be possible, you were injured in combat, received a combat Purple Heart Medal, were discharged from the National Guard for mental medical reasons after the Kent State shooting, have all kinds of social impairments, and were only rated with a 30 percent service-connected condition? This does not add up!' He had me sign up with the Disabled American Veterans organization and between the two of them, I was granted my entitled 100 percent service-connected compensation.

"Everything in my life started looking brighter and I met my second spouse, Barbara, who saw the money from the 100 percent as an opportunity to live higher in life. Her girl-friend is married to a 100 percent-disabled veteran, with a whole lot more serious service-connected disabilities, who also receives aid and attendance and other compensation. Within a year Barbara had accumulated more than $97,000 in credit card debts and none of these expenditures were for me. My daughter Mary found out about the abuse and as her grandmother would have done, she took charge. Mary and I had been estranged for years and I welcomed her back into my life. She worked as an administrative assistant in an attorney's office and knew people who could make things happen. After she found out the accumulative credit card debt was mostly spent on Barbara's children from a previous marriage, including the purchase of a vehicle for her daugh-ter, Mary's attorney friend presented an argument of a possi-bility of exploitation of a veteran to Barbara and she agreed quickly on a divorce."

Edward was elated his daughter was just like her grand-mother; she took charge and made things happen. He bought a beautiful, newly built four-bedroom home in a gated com-munity for his daughter, her spouse, three children, grand-daughter, and great-grandson. He paid all expenses for the dwelling, plus a new Cadillac Escalade SUV for his daughter. One of Mary's co-workers had a mother who was a widow. The two of them decided it would be great if Mary's father and this girlfriend's mother got married. They arranged the meeting and time to spend together before marriage.

This was my second visit, a follow-up visit. Edward was deemed incompetent for VA purposes for his inability to manage his financial affairs. During his compensation and pension examination he explained to the VA examiner he did not manage his funds; that his spouses, and now his daughter, took care of the money matters. Edward had trusted me, confided, and shared his deepest life stories and now I was witnessing some semblance of exploitation again. It was like being between a big rock and a very hard place. I first addressed my concerns with his daughter Mary whom we had appointed as the veteran's fiduciary payee, to manage his funds on behalf of the government. I knew Mary might have believed she understood her way around the laws, working in a law firm or acquainted with attorneys who would find ways to interpret the law and argue in court. Mary explained, "It is my father's money to do whatever he wants to do, and I cannot tell him not to do the thing that makes him feel good about himself. We have been estranged for a long time and he wasn't there during my struggles, so he believes it is something he wants to do." I first addressed the fact that it was not the veteran's money; the money was for him to have the best quality of life possible, not something to be used to mend old fences. The government could never pay him to be the man he was after the Marine Corps boot camp. Therefore, everyone has to pay his or her fair share, and I had to replace her as a fiduciary payee because her ability to manage her father's finances was questionable. I had apologized for having to share the government's position, and asked her not to "shoot the messenger," appreciating the trust that we had garnered. She was the voice and mind of a reasonable person and the VA did not deem her father could make reasonable decisions, being rated incompetent for VA purposes. The case was referred to the VA General Counsel for their review and action. The veteran and his new spouse continue to live a honeymoon life. This was a match made in heaven.

CHAPTER SEVEN

An Airman's Story of the Pearl Harbor Attack that Changed His World

"From the world wars of Europe to the jungles of the
Far East, from the deserts of the Middle East to the African
continent, and even here in our own hemisphere, our
veterans have made the world a better place and America
the great country we are today."
– U. S. Senator John Hoeven

"I was not known to be a man of faith, but surviving the Japanese attack on Pearl Harbor, Hawaii, was in God's hands. I had to believe I was covered in the blood of Jesus to survive the early Sunday morning attack on December 7, 1941," John said with unquestionable conviction. He went on to say, "More than 2,300 killed and 1,200 wounded and I had only suffered hearing damage and minor bumps and scratches from falling flat on my face in a pile of debris as I dove into a bomb crater. It was a miracle. As we ran for cover, bullets whistled past us from low-flying enemy fighter aircraft, bombers, and torpedo planes in two waves, launched from six aircraft carriers, killing the person running alongside me. I can vividly remember the line of tracer bullets going behind us as we ran for cover. I learned later, I was one of just eleven people who survived that attack in the area where I was assigned. It was only because I found a manhole and crawled inside the hole. The manhole was truly my safe haven. Bullets, fragments, and bodies fell on the cover and blood dripped down into the manhole. Each sound terrified me as I firmly held on to the ladder rail in the manhole, which was getting slippery from the blood leaking in. It seemed like forever until I stopped hearing aircraft flying over, bombs bursting in the air, the ground exploding above, and I finally decided to go up top. I struggled to get the cover off with the weight of bodies on top of it, but somehow I found the strength to make it happen. There were bodies everywhere, even floating on the water's edge—and the harbor was on fire."

John's recollection of that day and the subsequent days in his life was astonishing and a compelling, indescribable experience for me as I sat there listening. It appeared as if those moments were truly etched in his mind forever. Especially when he started talking of getting up that Sunday morning, a day he was only going into work for a couple of hours to do some final paperwork. He said, "I was walking from my barracks down to Pearl Harbor when my life flashed in front of me and my world changed. I was reborn; something or someone overtook me. After struggling out of the manhole, witnessing the aftermath of the attack on the way to my post in between Hangars 9 and 13, someone shouted, 'Here they come again!' Everyone in that area took cover behind the big steel hangar doors. The aftermath was worse than what I had initially witnessed coming out of the manhole. I was told eight U.S. Navy battleships were damaged, with four being sunk. Two of the four sunk were raised, and six of the total repairable. The Japanese also sank or damaged three cruisers, three destroyers, an anti-aircraft training ship, and a mine-layer. The aircraft on the air base were destroyed as they were lined up perfectly and used as targets for the attack. The U.S. bases and facilities in the Pacific had been placed on alert on multiple occasions; the officials doubted Pearl Harbor would be the first target. The intelligence reports claimed the Philippines would be attacked first. The intelligence community believed the threat on the air bases throughout the other countries and the naval base at Manila posed a greater threat to the sea-lanes and the shipment of supplies to Japan from territory to the south. They also assumed Japan was not capable of mounting more than one major naval operation at a time. This is why the attack caught us off-guard, crippling our abilities to defend ourselves or counter-attack the Japanese.

"The trucks filed with the dying and wounded parked in a circle in an effort of protection as portrayed in the old movies. Most of these trucks were completely demolished, only about seven men were still alive, despite the fact someone had taken a bed sheet, painted a large red cross on it and made it visually apparent. It was only a big target for the enemy fighter aircraft to shoot. The new hospital at Hickam AFB had limited capacity and could not accommodate all the dead, dying, and wounded. Therefore, most of the wounded were taken to Tripler, the Army hospital at Fort Shafter, which had expanded their capacity to accommodate about 1,000 beds.

"I volunteered to drive a truck over to Tripler, dodging debris and bodies along the road, listening to men crying in pain, smelling smoke in the air, tasting the gunpowder, and watching the devastation. The most interesting thing about that moment was that we had been on full alert for two weeks, but the Saturday before the attack, the alert was lifted. It seemed as if the commanders were expecting something to happen, but did not believe it would be at Pearl Harbor. No one was allowed to leave the base during the alert. Most of us felt if we were to go to war, it would be with the Russians. These are moments I live and see over and over. This is a time in my life that gives me strength and purpose to live with every day."

Somehow, some way, the Honolulu Star-Bulletin was able to publish an extra eight-page edition on Sunday, December 7, 1941, that read, "WAR! OAHU BOMBED BY JAPANESE PLANES. Six known dead, 21 injured, at emergency hospital; Attack Made on Island's Defense Area; Hundreds See City Bombed; Schools Closed and Names of Dead and Injured." The Associated Press by Transpacific Telephone: "San Francisco, Dec. 7. –President Roosevelt announced this morning that Japanese planes had attacked Manila and Pearl Harbor." I read the articles in his old Honolulu Star-Bulletin, which at that time did not completely recognize or address the gravity and world impact of the attacks from those Rising Sun emblems on the wing tips of those Japanese planes.

John said, "I was within thirty days of my Expiration Term of Service (ETS)—to be exact—ten days. I had an agreement for employment with Pan American Airlines as an aircraft mechanic. On the separation orders on the wall, marked in big red letters was the word 'FIGMO—Forget it I Got My Orders.' You can understand: I was short, on my way home, and had little to no interest in anything other than my new career. President Franklin D. Roosevelt asked Congress to declare war on Japan and avowed, 'December 7, 1941, is a day which will live in infamy.' Therefore all military personnel's ETS were involuntarily extended." The agreement he had with Pan American was nullified and John's military service was extended indefinitely until further notice. John said, "When one door closes, it can open another one. Two years later, I successfully completed Officer Candidate School and became an aircraft maintenance officer for the remaining service commitment time."

Years after the war, job opportunities were hard to come by, but the GI Bill was a lifesaver. John attended an FAA-certified aviation maintenance management education program and upon completion he started working at General Electric Aircraft Engines. John said, "GE is a great company that offers excellent benefits and great opportunities. I worked for GE for more than twenty-five very successful years, made good money, had two wonderful children, was divorced twice, and a widower once—the mother of my son and daughter. Therefore considering VA compensation was never an option for me. I purchased a home under the GI Bill as well, with my first spouse. I always believed I received the gift of life. I don't think a full day has gone by without either hearing those voices, or seeing those body parts outside Hangars 9 and 13 after the attack, the bodies on top of the manhole cover, and those floating in the water. There are more deserving people than I needing those benefits."

John expressed his sadness with a report he had read and provided me with a copy to read. It was a VA article posted Wednesday, May 30, 2001: "In signing a law that will create a monument on the National Mall to the veterans of World War II, President George W. Bush said that there's no time to waste because a thousand of these veterans are dying every day."

"This meant there are not too many of us left to honor the service and sacrifice in the world's freedom as we honor those who lost their lives at Pearl Harbor." John also said, "I am very grateful to God for affording me the opportunity to live this long. If I knew I would have lived this long, I would have taken better care of myself. The privileged life I have had is unreal." He is 89 years old and suffers from the early stages of dementia as well as hearing loss, and resides in a licensed 50-bed assisted-living facility in a beautiful private room. The walls are well decorated with his military awards, pictures, and educational accomplishments, and he was very proud to share his story about each one of them.

John had a look of disgust on his face and said, "It was over 65 years after the war ended and with spouse number three, Rita, whom I should have never married," he openly admitted. "She insisted I get medical attention for her nonprofessional diagnosis of me suffering from depression caused by shell shock. Rita knew it all. She was a research registered nurse with GE, someone with all the answers. Rita claimed I had feelings of sadness, emptiness, and hopelessness because she could not get along with my kids. She also claimed I cried too often or too much, did not sleep well, and coupled with me being irritable, these were signs of shell shock, caused by the experience at Pearl Harbor. After her constant nagging, we visited a doctor who confirmed her theory and said I was suffering from depression. We had no idea what to do next after all these years since the war was over.

"The notion of the VA not having a published, disseminated entitlement program for the veterans' community, with details on how to obtain benefits and where to go, only angered Rita. She contacted a well-respected attorney she knew at a large law firm in the area, who explained how complicated VA law is and that none of his partners in the practice would get involved or take VA cases. It was shocking to us, but those were words I had heard previously as the perception of VA law."

I explained to John and his son John, Jr., also known as "Jack," how common it was in the legal community not to accept VA cases. John said, "One of the most aggravating things about Rita was her so-called 'badge of honor.' She would constantly repeat the story of breaking the clue of the VA bureaucratic puzzle. I was sick of hearing the story of her best friend who was caught up in the VA paper mill. Rita claimed that the perception of most people is that the VA hoped people would get frustrated and give up, and this is why it takes so long. The VA would request documents previously submitted, just to delay the processing of the claim. These documents are easily assessable under the VA's so-called, 'Duty to Assist' program. Rita's girlfriend's spouse died on active duty in the war and she was receiving VA surviving spouse benefits for years until she met and married a man she thought was so wonderful. After twenty-two years of marriage, they were divorced and she was experiencing some financial hardship in life. During a casual conversation with Rita, she shared her story. Rita had read an article in a magazine explaining how Congress had passed a bill authorizing a prior Death Indemnity Compensation (DIC) recipient the opportunity of reinstatement to their first spouse's benefits. The next day Rita forcibly escorted her friend to the local Regional Office and provided the documents she was told to have when she contacted the 1-800 number for assistance. These were documents required for the reinstatement of DIC. A year after filing for the DIC reinstatement, she relocated to Florida to assist her ailing parents. It was a win-win opportunity for her: She had limited funds and was caring for her parents. After several phone calls to the

Regional Office in Washington where she had filed the initial claim and had been told her claim was being processed, Rita drove six hours to the Regional Office in Florida with her best friend and luckily they had copies of the original documents submitted. The computer system showed there were no records of the claim. The VA representative at the Regional Office in St. Petersburg, Florida, accepted the documents and informed her he would forward the documents to Washington where the files were kept. Another three months went by, with several telephone calls to the 1-800 numbers and being told there was nothing in the computer system showing the claim had been submitted. Rita and her girlfriend made another six-hour drive to the Regional Office to request a meeting with the supervisor. She apologized for the inconveniences, updated the computer with the documents, and requested the files to be transferred to the Florida Regional Office. Three months later, after several phone calls to the St. Petersburg, Florida, Regional Office and being told the case was being processed, Rita wrote a letter and her girlfriend signed it, sent a copy to both her congressmen and senators. Three weeks later, Rita's girlfriend received a large sum of money and an award letter."

I informed them of some of the best places for assistance instead of driving those twelve hours to the Regional Office, as Rita and her girlfriend had done. These veterans service organizations—the Veterans of Foreign Wars, American Legion, American Veterans, Disabled American Veterans— all have representatives in the VA Regional Office buildings. The County Veterans Services Offices, which are listed in the local telephone books, can assist with expediting the claims and the whole VA Regional Office staff is accountable. I also expressed my disappointment with some of the attorneys whose behaviors I perceived to be illegal, unethical, and non-supportive. But there are some real devoted attorneys or retired military Judge Advocate General (JAG) Officers who understand the system and would work hard for the beneficiary-entitled benefits.

I also shared the story of an attorney who was required to do some community service as part of the prerequisite for her scholarship. She chose a homeless shelter. One veteran frequented the shelter for food and a warm bed a couple of times during her visit. She alleged he adopted her as his "little blue-eyed sister." She claimed to have had no knowledge of his financial status. The veteran was entitled to a sizeable amount of VA compensation and Social Security benefits, which was very attractive, in my assumption, to a second-year law student. She became good friends with this veteran. She would bail him out of jail when he was arrested for loitering or vagrancy, and in turn he would loan her money to pay her bills, which he proudly admitted. For her graduation from law school, he bought her a new SUV. As a gesture of good faith she established a refuge, offering room and board at a farmhouse in the rural part of town for him and nine other 100-percent-disabled veterans with Social Security benefits. She convinced all of them it was their safe haven, a place off the streets with everything taken care of, and in their best interest.

During my initial visit with this veteran, she appeared to be very protective and I had no idea as to why. Months later I went back to visit another veteran at this place, and the business office manager informed me of phone calls the veteran had been receiving from two people claiming to be his children. The attorney had listed him as having no next of kin on all available documents, including the VA records. The business office manager was not sure what to do, since the attorney denied the request of the veteran's children to visit. She gave me their phone numbers and I contacted his children only to find out they had other siblings. The attorney had been telling them for years, "He did not want to see or hear from them. The courts had appointed her as the guardian of person and property; she is his protector and the enforcer of the law. Trying to contact him is an unwanted act, same as a stalker in the court of law." The veteran's mother was seriously ill and her wishes were for his kids to see him. I was discovering that the attorney was living high on behalf of several disabled veterans and some others around town. She gave them $100 a week for incidental spending and allegedly paid all their other expenses. The attorney had the veteran sign a notarized statement saying, "upon his death all his financial assets will go to me for the years of service to him." This statement was allegedly signed before the veteran was deemed incompetent. She also had a Durable Power of Attorney, coupled with a will of the veteran with an affidavit, giving the attorney everything the veteran owns at the time of his death." The attorney had noted in the will, "He had no known living relative."

Through the assistance of the VA Medical Outreach Program, the American Legion organization assisted this veteran to obtain a large sum of money from a ten-year pending appeal, which was over $250,000. The attorney had invested these funds during the booming real estate era and the veteran had done very well. So did she, by illegally claiming and receiving a 5 percent fee of his total annual income for services rendered.

It was common practice for her to invest these veterans' funds in investment areas where she deemed it would maximize their investment and she would receive her 5 percent monthly or an annual fee. I immediately terminated her service and forwarded the case to the VA general counsel with a request to have a copy of the report or a summary forwarded to the State Legal Board of Ethics for their review and actions. I also contacted and appointed a professional guardian as custodian-in-fact, pending his appointment as successor guardian by the courts.

Back to John's story, his son Jack claimed to be unaware of the struggles his father had experienced initially. John said, "Rita was like a 'bulldog,' a natural, instinctive, and persistent healthcare professional, from her nurses' training. She refused to deny her so-called belief of any professional legal steward of the law, not accepting VA claims. Therefore, she contacted the state legal board and expressed her concerns. The board provided her with a list of board-certified attorneys in the state and she contacted an attorney in Miami-Dade County. It was more than eighteen months before I received the awarded 40 percent service-connected disability. Rita was very proud of her accomplishment, claiming she could make things happen and I was a disabled veteran," he explained apologetically. He said, "I did not need the money and I know many of those WWII, Korean, and Vietnam era veterans could use the money more than I. The excellent benefits at the General Electric Aircraft Engines Company were great and I had it all."

The $3,200 monthly room and board cost at the assisted-living facility, plus a couple hundred for medications, other medical services, and the incidentals, had depleted most of John's lifelong savings. "The assisted-living facility marketing director was a beacon of light for the family in obtaining assistance to supplement the depleting funds," said Jack. The marketing director crunched the numbers and figured we could not get from here to there without some additional assistance. She arranged the meeting with a member of the American Veterans (AMVETS) organization, which was a godsend. "He had an encyclopedic knowledge of the best options for my Pop," said Jack. "This gentleman from the AMVETS office had been a Veterans' Service Representative, knew the VA system, and was willing to devote the time in making sure my Pop received the best deal, is truly a testimony to what my Pop has always advocated. He assisted my Pop to complete the forms and documents for a VA Improved Pension with Aid and Attendance, as a greater benefit over the awarded service-connected 40 percent disability, with a pending requested increase for secondary conditions. The difference was almost twice as much, the waiting time was only nine months, and the amount of out-of-pocket expenses for my sister and me were a lot less.

"My Pop always claimed to have a guardian angel looking over him, despite the situation or crazy decisions he was forced to make, somehow, some way, things would always work out for the best. In the twilight of his life, it is not uncommon for him to reflect on his childhood, military days, career choices, and the regrettable decisions of marrying his second and third spouses. But he would always talk about our mother as his best friend and partner who gave him the best two children any man could dream of having, before she died. She had been his rock."

Jack also said, "The money my sister and I will be paying to ensure our Pop has the best quality of life, until the day the good Lord calls him home, is only a token and not enough money to pay him back for the life he's affording us or life we had the privilege of having. Our father is a humble man who made a difference in the world, both personally and professionally, and we are very proud to be his children with profound appreciation for the honor."

CHAPTER EIGHT

The Draft Will Never Socially Or Politically Define Me

"Caring for veterans shouldn't be a partisan issue.
It should be an American one."

– JENNIFER GRANHOLM,
FORMER GOVERNOR OF MICHIGAN

It was 1943, another heavy, rainy spring day in West Virginia, and Lester's father, Luther, stopped in their local post office for the family mail. It was a shock to see his son had received a letter from their local Selective Service Board. He realized this letter could have been as a result of his lack of political affiliation; not being a part of the local political party and not paying the county $4.00 voting tax may have been the county's retaliation. When Lester returned home and opened his mail, it was a notice for him to report for compulsory military service, the draft, with a greeting from the United States president, the commander-in-chief, through the local Selective Service Board. The family's presumption of the Selective Service's act of reprisal truly angered his father to no end, because two of Lester's brothers were in the military, serving overseas. He was only 18 years old, and it was understood, he was the son destined to take care of his mother, if anything happened to their father. The family was very proud of the other two sons who were members of the Armed Forces. Their mother, Elizabeth, had her sons' branch of service decals and flags displayed on their front window indicating her sons were serving overseas. This patriotic symbolism act was known as a "mother's pride" to the nation. Lester said, "To the best of my knowledge, none of my fellow classmates had received draft notices right after graduation. I was the first 18-year-old inductee in this county. Some of my classmates were drafted two years later. The most interesting or disheartening part of this chain of events was that none of these classmates had served a day overseas or in the war."

Luther tried to prove reprisal against the Selective Service Board, but it was impossible. It was like fighting the White House. Everyone knew and would often question his family's political affiliation as a way to neutralize the conversation. He tried talking with anyone who would listen, with negative results. Everyone apologized, but claimed not to be able to do anything for him. Most people knew each other, or were a part of the good old boys' club. But those who were not a part of the chosen circle of friends were outsiders in the county. Politics in Lester's family household was not something he had the nerve to discuss. The foremost concern in their home was living from one day to next, with some food on the table. He explained how he lived most of his life believing his father's early death was as a result of the self-imposed stress, believing his son had to go to war because of his political affiliation. Lester then assumed the responsibilities of support for his mother. Everyone extended his or her sympathy and the President said, "This country needs you." It was very hard for Lester to get over believing what he perceived to be a political injustice that society had legislated on those deemed to be a lower class, politically or socially, so he fulfilled his legal obligation and reported for the draft.

However, Lester later admitted, "It was one of the best decisions I had made in my life." Looking back, he claimed to be totally convinced it was the right one. But the military way of life was not an occupation he could have made a career. The military was not for everyone and surely not for him, he admitted. The three years of obligatory military service, extended because of the war, was something that eventually made him proud. To actually see what was happening in the world was invaluable. Too much was happening in the war in Europe and Japan for the military to let him go home at his Expiration Term of Service (ETS). Therefore, he was involuntarily extended while he was actively and physically involved in the war in Europe.

Now at the age of 86, he feels wiser and proud to have lived this long, even though he has several service-connected disabilities. Although he feels like a hostage to all the medications required for the best quality of life, Lester said, "I am very happy with the hand I was dealt, because the alternative, death, was worse than being a hostage to medications. No one has come back from death other than Jesus Christ with a better explanation. I am proud to admit." He had four seven-day pill organizers for thirty days. Morning, noon, evening, and bedtime for every day of the week sat on his kitchen table, across from their refrigerator. He also had a small pill container to carry a daily dose, if needed. It was his explanation of the commitment to staying as healthy as possible with the prescribed medications necessary to maintain his health.

Lester's face lit up when he said, "It was so surreal to go to the movie and watch the first draftee of the county on scene, how proud he appeared to have been drafted with all the good things about the war in the world." But bitterness of the selective service system and the way he had been treated because his parents were not a part of the social circle of friends and the political environment of that time had plagued his mind. The thought of this area is so vivid and still angers him more now than ever. He refused to allow his anger to define or control his character. He tried to make the best choices in his life without allowing those memories as an obstacle; instead moving forward in life. In Lester's world, it was not who you were or what you were, at only eighteen years old, and from a poor family. It was how best to survive in this harsh world, in spite of your humble beginnings. His personal conviction in life was to etch his character as a human being in the minds of those who deemed the need to regulate people into a social class beneath them. He struggled for years with the thoughts of being a victim of society and refused to ever be class-defined by anyone else. He realizes now, how that time in his life was truly a good teaching opportunity that he learned to accept. The sense of gratitude he expressed in his voice and on his face was priceless, as he shared this part of his journey in life.

The pride of serving in the United States Armed Forces and going to war was a feeling Lester found very difficult to explain. Going into his "I Love Me Room" with all his awards, decorations, and commendations around him, he shared his feelings of excitement after completing the Basic Combat Training and Advanced Individual Training. He had the opportunity of going overseas and being a part of history and serving this country as a privilege. He felt so confident, having been trained with the best of the best in the world, by the most knowledgeable team-building instructors any young man could dream of having. Lester described the M36 tank destroyer as the best war machine in the world during that time and here he was, a young man from West Virginia, in control of such a war-changing destroyer. He was anxious and could not wait to apply the knowledge and training he had received to show the world how great the M36 tank destroyer was. The look on his face as he showed the picture of himself on top of the tank was indescribable.

Before leaving for his assignment overseas, Lester was granted 15 days' furlough, which at the time he was not too excited about, other than spending a couple days with his mother. He could not stop talking about the world's best machine the Army had trained him on, the M36 tank destroyer with the 90mm gun. Then his 15 days were extended to 45 days because of the non-availability of troop ships to transport the soldiers to Europe.

Lester was very grateful for the delay after he met the most beautiful lady he ever had the privilege of meeting—his soul mate. He was head-over-heels in love, at first sight, with Roberta. At the time the two got married, she was sixteen and he nineteen. They have been married for the last sixty-eight years with one adult son and three grandchildren. Roberta stayed at home with her parents while her spouse went to war. She described the eleven months and fifteen days Lester spent in the war zone as the longest days ever, which seemed like years, especially to a newlywed, a high school senior, who was still living with her parents. Lester was also proud to admit how Roberta has always been his lifeline. The reason he was able to manage all the struggles after the war and the clinical behavioral conditions throughout the years was solely because of that sixteen-year-old girl. But Roberta also had some serious medical problems throughout the years. The strength of love the two appeared to relish after so many years is a gift. Especially when they openly admitted with such profound conviction of not believing they could live through life without each other. The passion on their faces spoke volumes of what a lifelong love story is all about.

During our visit, Roberta sat at the dining room table across from me while Lester sat at the head of the table. Roberta looked at Lester with such pride. This is the man she fell in love with, two weeks after meeting him. The most gratifying thing to Roberta was the fact that Lester was talking about his days in the war. She recalled the devastated lives they shared when Lester first came back from the war and refused to talk about his nightmares or anything about his time in Europe. It was amazing to her how willing her spouse was to share his military journey when he found out I was a Vietnam veteran. This is something Lester claimed was personal. He said, "I could not imagine coming back home from a war zone and be treated the way the Vietnam veterans were mistreated when they came home." It appeared as if it was a bridge he has lived to cross. Something he kept within all these years and this was the key that opened the door. The inner depth of his suppressed emotions after the war and his imagination of the struggles Vietnam veterans were subjected to was not something he could live through. His gratitude was greatly appreciated by both his spouse and me.

He assured Roberta he would never do anything stupid like kill himself, because he knows this is not what she wants him to do. He openly asked her not to ever think of such a ridiculous thought herself. He then explained his flattering reason, why he felt such a personal connection/trust with me and yet with none of the other VA employees he met throughout the years. Lester said, "What this man does is not a job, it is a passion. He understands and connects with the veterans." In an effort to change the current environment and redirect the tone of the conversation, I questioned the journey he had highlighted on a map on the wall.

It was the right question at the right time. Lester said without missing a beat, "The troop ship voyage to Great Britain was my first trip out of the United States and one I will never forget, especially how sick everyone became during the trip. The best outcome of the journey to Great Britain was to arrive and learn that all of our equipment had not arrived with the ship. It was not expected in theater for another ten days; therefore, everyone had ten days to recuperate. But to most, after traveling this far, so long, enduring such a journey, the trust and friendship in each other developed during training on their duties and responsibilities, coupled with the anticipation of the war and strong desire to bring about the destruction of the German war machine, had gotten the best of them."

Lester explained the greater power he learned to appreciate, is something bigger than life. Even now he is unable to explain it in words. It was like an omen that someone was looking out for him, he said, because after the equipment finally arrived and they were about to leave England for France, "We only took summer clothing; the presumption was the war was close to an end and the troops would not need their winter clothing, so why take them?" His platoon would be joining the 1st Canadian Army with the 4th Infantry Division. They lived to regret not taking the winter clothing during the bitter winter that followed.

By the time they got to Utah Beach as the third wave, the two Navy ships had pulled up as close as possible to shore to bomb everything that did not move on the top of the ridge of the hill, and protect the landing troops. The first and second wave had suffered a great deal of casualties and death by the time the third wave landed. He described the first and only casualty of the third wave as stupidity. A young nineteen-year-old kid, who had left his secured position without the all-clear command, was killed running from one side to the other in the open. Lester explained how he still sees this kid's face, hears his voice, and wonders why he was so stupid. He said, "I had just turned twenty and to this day I don't know why so many people around me died and I did not. Perhaps, this is why during quiet times I hear things no one else hears or sees, with those nightmares of those who gave the ultimate sacrifice for us all."

Standing in his "I Love Me Room" looking at his big map he had on the wall, displaying the place of disembarkation and the journey from one end of Europe to the other, and listening to him describe in detail each day or place of battle, beginning with the dreadful day, June 6, 1944, and the first time he saw bodies, lots of body parts laying on the beach, or having to shoot at someone who was shooting at them. He continued his description of vicious fighting as they marched into Reims, through Brussels, Antwerp, Maastricht, back down to Aachen, Eschweiler into Cologne—lots of death, killing, capturing key posts, and moving on until they got to Munich—it was as if he were still there and I alongside of him. He shared an array of feelings during that vivid trip through his memorable journey. He remembered joining forces with the newly established 104th Division in Cologne with a commanding officer committed to minimizing the fog of war—being killed by friendly fire—which the commanding officer had perfected in Africa. They would engage the enemy by night, without loaded weapons, but with grenades. Any weapon that went off was the enemy's, while his platoon only used grenades to kill or capture the enemy. This tactic allowed them to capture more territories and prisoners of war than any other division in the U.S. Army. Those ninety-five consecutive days of active combat were described as brutal. It was kill or be killed and destroy every- or anything that may get in the way, cause harm, or impede the mission. Lester claimed it was reported the 692 Tank Destroyer Battalion was part of capturing 2,492 prisoners and apprehending a Gestapo agent who was the first spy executed by the Seventh Army. He recalled joining the 14th Armed Division in the south of France after they had suffered a heavy loss, about half or more of the division were killed or wounded. His platoon was the lead strike force and for that effort he received the Legion of Honor. They had driven the last Germans out of France and greatly contributed to the United States' decisive role in the liberation of France. Lester stood with such pride as he identified the letter on the wall and read each word with conviction from the President of the French Republic. It had been presented to him by the Ambassador of France on June 3, 2008. Lester continued to talk of his journey as if it was yesterday, with such pride that it would be sad not to share his story with the world. Especially when Roberta said, "Thank you, this is the best therapeutic moment Lester has had in years, that I have witnessed." She spoke with such love for the man she married as a child and struggled through their sacrifices, illnesses, sadness, and joyful moments as a badge of honor. It was a very emotional moment. I, too, had to control my emotions. She remembered how hard it was for him to get or keep a job after being discharged from the military. He had six different employments in six months after returning from the war. They went from place to place, until he finally got a job in Michigan, which he kept until he retired thirty-five years later.

He described every journey as factually as possible, but would often apologize for not remembering the intimate details of things by saying, "my computer shorts out every now and then." His spouse, Roberta, would look at him with such a special look, somehow the computer would reboot and everything continue. After the interview, Lester and Roberta said the local Bob Evans restaurant had the best banana bread in the county. They volunteered to show me where it was. Upon arrival, his spouse said, "Lester remembers everything about his military service in detail, but could not remember to change his shoes." He was still wearing his house slippers, standing in front of the restaurant. It was clear Lester was slipping a little bit, his short-term memories were not the best and he would apologize for it or rationalize it. At first he didn't quite remember what day of the week it was and he simply said, "When you are retired and have lived this long, time does not matter because it comes and goes every day we wake up. I am so happy to have my best friend with me and thank God for another day with her in my life. She is my strength, lifeline, and reason for living during the war and every day after. Believe me, she is as pretty as the first time my eyes ever saw such a beauty."

Among Lester's deep confession of his appreciation for the woman he has shared his life with all these years, Roberta had to keep it real. She said, "The most confusing to both Lester and me is to understand why despite the mental, physical, and emotional trauma Lester had endured, which include those torturous moments in the bitter cold with summer clothing and frostbitten feet; or his continuing to see those bodies in the railroad cars or lying on the ground (the pictures stored in his scrapbook); the constant scent of bodies in the railroad cars which are so real to him, night after night, yet Veterans Affairs deems these issues not likely a result of his combat experiences. It makes things very hard on me as his spouse, especially when he can't go to sleep and he is up all hours of the night. He has problems remembering recent things, and has severe obsessive rituals, locking the doors with the key and checking them several times, compulsive about doing things the same way all the time, a creature of obsessive habits." Roberta insisted I have a copy of the spouse's statement in support of the veteran's claim as a result of constant denial of claim for medical evidence or continuity of care for PTSD after years of delays. She said in her letter, "It truly saddens me to see what my spouse of sixty-eight years has become in recent years. Lester and I were married very young and he went off to the war at a young age to fight for this country. He returned home from the war and refused to talk about all the atrocities he had endured. Lester would often say, 'What goes on overseas we should try our best to forget and move on in life. It was for the world's freedom.'

"Lester always says he received the greatest gift, life. He personally witnessed the death of others or loss of their extremities. He has been very adamant about not requesting benefits or anything from anyone. It was very clear he strongly believed there were many other veterans who needed it more than we did. He recently shared the real root cause of not seeking medical attention as a result of the medic in the

VA hospital who insulted or made him feel less than a man for addressing his medical atrocities. What a travesty for my spouse, Lester, our hero, and this sad medic who had never served a day in the war or witnessed the things Lester had, like killing or risking being killed. I have also witnessed on numerous occasions after the war, people asking; 'How many people have you shot or killed?' Lester would say, 'They were shooting, I shot back and they stopped shooting.' He hated to talk about the war or the things he had to do to survive and only kept it inside. The things he shared with you were truly amazing and uncharacteristic of the man I know. I thank you for allowing us that precious moment."

Roberta went on to say, "I am not sure of the value of this statement, but I believe I have a moral commitment to share my personal observation of the chronic adjustment disorder experience with Lester for the last sixty-eight years. It should be clear to any reasonable person how protective/guarded he has been of his personal life, being in denial of his medical condition or believing there are veterans who need benefits more than us. I am not a physician, but I do know Lester suffers from PTSD with all the symptoms, especially when we think of what he endured for 195 consecutive days in the war. Therefore your assistance in doing the right things right will be greatly appreciated."

Lester is like most veterans of his era, WWII, who were very proud to have served and truly believe coming back home with all their body parts was a gift and a privilege. They did not want any handouts and they believe there are lots of other people who need these benefits more than they do. Therefore, seeking their entitled benefits would never be a part of their makeup. But as the numbers of veterans of that era are whittling down and reunions are more precious, people are urging each other to ascertain their benefits. They share names and numbers of service organizations that are willing to assist them. But Lester is very grateful for the little compensation benefit he is receiving, even after so many years of denials. We should honor the service of our veterans and reward the damage imposed on those great and humble men, but sadly enough, too many veterans have died before receiving their entitled benefit as a result of the lack of urgency in processing these heroes' claims.

Lester shared a neighbor's story, an eighty-eight-year-old Airborne Ranger combat veteran whose claim after 26 months was granted at 60 percent service-connected disability with several claims being deferred for more medical evidence. His payment was withheld pending an appointment of a spouse payee for the last eleven months since the spouse signed and agreed on waiving the 60-days due process period. No word has been received to date. The veteran was deemed incompetent for VA purposes. Several of the veteran's more serious medical conditions have worsened and despite all the letters the family has sent to the director and service center manager at the VA Regional Office with not even an acknowledgment. Who can blame family members when they start to believe that the VA is thinking, "If the veteran dies perhaps the case will go away"? If not, it will be another journey to receive funds for bills the spouse had incurred as a result of the veteran's illness. The process is not customer friendly; instead it is another goat rope the beneficiaries are subjected to.

The forgotten legacies, sacrifices, and broken promises veterans are subjected to were issues Lester gracefully addressed as something he hoped his story could minimize.

How can anyone enjoy the freedom and privileges given by hundreds of thousands of veterans and yet continue to stall their very legitimate benefit requests? Veterans and their families believe that their claim files are being put aside, with redundant requests for medical evidence or documents previously submitted, to wait until the veteran dies before awarding the benefits.

The VA must minimize the continuation of any behavior that maintains these beliefs. The "Level Three Priority" offer to "veterans over 70 years of age" should include those veterans with known terminal medical conditions and triage teams should urgently process our heroes' cases.

CHAPTER NINE

A Witness of Society's Transformation

"The willingness of America's veterans to sacrifice for our
country has earned them our lasting gratitude."
– U. S. REPRESENTATIVE JEFF MILLER

The draft and the Vietnam Conflict, a couple of political and social hot potatoes, had polarized the country. Baby boomers sought exemptions and deferments, left the country via Canada or South America, or filed for Conscientious Objector status on the grounds of moral or religious principles, based on politics, expediency, or self-interest. Politicians were very vocal on their views as a platform for their elections or reelection.

Organized protests all over the country were some indication of the country's disfavor toward the Vietnam War. Crude and insensitive demonstrative behavior toward the men and women who had served was common. It was truly a sad time for the members of the Armed Forces, who were serving, putting their lives on the line, or even giving the ultimate sacrifice for the world's freedom, and yet the society seemed oblivious. It is in stark contrast to the appreciation for the veterans of today's wars.

Vietnam was the only conflict in America's history that was never declared a war. President John F. Kennedy's decision to send more military troops to Vietnam as "advisors" had never been changed. President Dwight D. Eisenhower had previously committed 900 U.S. troops as advisors, which resulted in approximately 211,450 military casualties—those dead or wounded—at the end of the conflict in 1975.

We were treated unfairly when we came home or when we read some of the unacceptable stories in the *Stars and Stripes* newspaper while on the ground in Vietnam. As a naïve kid from the Panama Canal Zone, I could not comprehend, if President Kennedy said, "American friends of Vietnam, Burma, Thailand, India, Japan, the Philippines, Laos, and Cambodia are amongst those whose security would be threatened if the Red Tide of Communism overflowed into Vietnam," why were so many American people so angry? We were only following orders as directed by the Commander-in-Chief. We heard, "President Lyndon B. Johnson was not sure why he committed troops to that war." Then President Richard M. Nixon said, "There were no troops in Laos or Cambodia in May 1970," and students were shot at Kent State University in protest of the war. Veterans who were in Laos and Cambodia were shocked as they told their stories of disappointment with the political betrayal, but each and every one of us had either sworn or affirmed to obey the orders of the President of the United States in accordance with the Uniform Code of Military Justice (UCMJ).

It is very common to observe travelers in the airports in America today clapping or extending their appreciation with the words "thank you for your service" to troops. This gesture of appreciation is for their contributions and sacrifices for this nation's security and freedom. Today's attitude of most Americans is that the men and women are serving this country and they are eager to show their appreciation. In reality these service members are keeping America free and the world safe for democracy. Children and grandchildren of those dissenting baby boomers are now service members who stand guard around the world to keep wars off of our shores. What a remarkable transformation of society today.

One cold winter morning in January 2011 on the way back from North Carolina visiting my daughter, my granddaughter, and my mother, we stopped at a Cracker Barrel in Savannah, Georgia, for breakfast. My spouse, Laurie, and I saw a young man enter the restaurant dressed in his army combat uniform (ACUs). He sat across the aisle from us and ordered breakfast, and as usual, I engaged this young man in a conversation. He shared how he had just returned from Iraq on his way home, but this was his first stop since he was longing for a real American breakfast, including a double order of deep-fried bacon. He said, "It is my third tour in that theater and I am proud to be back home receiving the appreciation and love that I have received." I could not have been prouder of the apparent transformation in society at that moment. Watching several patrons walk by and thank him for his service to the world was remarkable. Quietly I contacted the waitress, while my spouse continued with the conversation, and offered to pay for his meal. The waitress informed me that two ladies sitting in back of him had already paid for his meal long before anyone else had even considered it.

When he walked in and sat at the table, I could not help but think of my cousin Jack who had just returned from Afghanistan a few days prior, after his second trip to that theater in Kuwait and Afghanistan. He shared his proudest moment as a member on active duty in the National Guard. During a sad flight to another cousin's funeral in San Francisco, the first words out of the check-in agent's mouth, when she realized my cousin was on active duty and returning from Afghanistan, was a warm welcome with a heart-filled, "thank you for our freedom." She then made an announcement offering all active duty military members a first-class seat. Jack explained he was unable to speak at that moment as a result of how emotional he had become. The faces of a couple of soldiers—who made the ultimate sacrifice for this freedom—flashed in front of him, and the tears started. Jack said, "I could only gesture an acceptance for the offer, I couldn't speak. The thoughts of those soldiers leaving Afghanistan in a casket draped with Old Glory got the best of me at that moment. I boarded the aircraft and everyone at the gate started applauding, and other passengers walking by toward their gates joined in and thanked me for my service. The acknowledgment did not end at the gate. I sat in my seat believing I had composed myself until most of the passengers expressed their appreciation as they walked past my seat. I was embarrassed for being a public spectacle. A First Sergeant in the U.S. Army displaying that type of public emotion is unacceptable. I am a leader and a leader leads with strength, not emotions. Not only was I treated royally; the unbelievable public respect for my chosen profession was incomprehensible and unexpected. The more love the passengers and airline staff showed, the clearer their faces appeared and the louder the last conversations of those soldiers rang in my head.

"I especially remembered my older brother Frank, a casualty during the 1968 Tet Offensive in Vietnam. Frank was severely injured in combat and spent two-and-a-half months at the Letterman Army Medical Center, located on the Presidio of San Francisco, California. He was ashamed of his service in Vietnam and disappointed with the type of public reception he and his fellow warriors received when they returned. I was the youngest child, just seven years old when my brother came home. For years, I could not comprehend why my big brother was ashamed to have gone to war and then labored through life as if it was such a burden. He was our hero for many reasons, aside from serving in Vietnam: a talented artist, vocalist, musician, and anything else he put his mind to be. Instead he chose to go into that closet and never come out. Frank never spoke about his tour in Vietnam, but he died from cancer as a result of the exposure to Agent Orange. These thoughts kept me grounded and did not allow me to act any more ridiculous in public." My cousin spoke with such an ambiguous feeling of the royal treatment he received from the airlines and the other passengers as well as those voices he hears and faces he sees. America now recognizes and accepts the sacrifices the Armed Forces are making for us all. The appreciation, recognition, and acknowledgment shared were sadly enough, denied most Vietnam veterans, as a result of the public opinion or political agendas back home. "My brother Frank, our real hero, has died and was never afforded the recognition for his contributions towards world peace," said Jack.

In June 1971 after a long flight from Cam Ranh Bay, Republic of Vietnam, where the base had been under attack as my plane was taking off, I was terrified, believing I was so close, yet might not make it back home alive. I had heard stories of GIs getting killed the last day or week in country and I had to believe it was not in God's plan for this to happen to me. I found myself praying to God, to not allow us to be that story told of the Viet Cong shooting and killing an aircraft full of returning GIs. I kept hearing my grandmother's words, "If you die in that forsaken place, I will die with you. I will just stop breathing until I die. This world is no place without you in it and I don't want to live without you."

Home, the United States, was called "the World" to most GIs. We finally landed back in the World, at Seattle-Tacoma International Airport, without any fanfare or welcoming acknowledgment. After going through customs and security, we waited around for an hour because the dogs found a bag of marijuana in someone's bag. Therefore, customs had to conduct a more thorough check of each returnee's bags. While walking through the airport in uniform, which was the only way to board the aircraft back home from Vietnam in those days, a couple of skinheads came up to me and spat in my face and called me a baby killer. I was truly confused, I concluded it was as a result of Lt. William Calley's massacre when he was found guilty of murdering twenty-two My Lai civilians, which had nothing to do with me. I vividly remembered how ashamed I was for serving in Vietnam and totally shocked that I allowed someone to disrespect me in this manner and had not knocked his lights out. But I had learned how to subdue my passion and how to manage my behavior, learning self-control early in my career. What now felt like decades ago, I had only been in the military three days and found myself in correctional custody for assaulting a non-commissioned officer. The drill sergeant had kicked me in my butt and I knocked him out. This warranted a twenty-one-day trip to the correctional custody facility. Now taking my first steps on American soil, I remember how angry I felt, being publicly disrespected, feeling hopeless, and unable to understand what gave anyone the right to do something like that to me. It saddened me to believe the most powerful country in the world was so out of control, that society condoned such behavior from their citizens; especially when I reflected on the number of young men and women who came back in pine boxes or missing body parts as a result of the war for freedom. The country did not know or appreciate what each and every one of us had endured for their rights to be free. Many of the veterans were hooked on marijuana laced with opium, finding respite after shooting someone for the first time, or watching comrades die—sometimes in their arms, or seeing someone right next to you get shot. We made sacrifices for world peace and we truly believed it would make the world a better place for everyone. Not just so some could feel free to disrespect us for their belief with no regards of us doing the job we were ordered to do.

I was sickened to return to the land of the free with spitting and name-calling as my welcome. No one prepared us for such a heartbroken, disappointing homecoming. I went into the men's room, took off my battle dress uniform (BDUs) and put them in the trash. I was one of many Vietnam vets who never talked or openly admitted to having served in Vietnam, for years. Our service to the world never ends at the end of the military campaign. Those demons are life-long and may affect the veteran or their families forever. We carried shame or guilt for having served in a war many Vietnam veterans believed to have been a useless war when the country appeared not to appreciate our sacrifices. The deep and silent guilt of coming home, not knowing why someone you believe to be more worthy of life than you had to die; the way so many came home injured and to see their faces or hear their voices, believing each one had much more to offer the world than I. Hugging a fellow Vietnam vet and whispering the words "Welcome Home" is without question a confirmation we appreciate who we are and what we sacrificed.

Today, I am a casualty of exposure to the herbicide Agent Orange. In April 2009 diabetes mellitus, and in June 2010, I was diagnosed with prostate cancer—two of the VA-conceded presumptive conditions associated with Agent Orange. Someone once shared another presumptive theory of Agent Orange: "It is not if, it is when."

The privilege of visiting other veterans from World War II, the Korean War, and Vietnam as a Department of Veterans Affairs employee enabled me to truly appreciate the value of our service to the world, keeping it safe for democracy. The pride each and every member of our armed forces and their families shared with such conviction and desired to let the world know. Many of them may not have known what day of the week it was, or what they had for lunch or breakfast, but they could speak vividly and account for every day in the military.

Many veterans or their family members felt it would be a disservice to the world not to share their stories of the United States being perceived as the world's police and peacekeepers. They claimed they found it very offensive to hear people address the military world commitment and humanitarian missions as world policing. Explaining the pride of making a remarkable difference in several great humanitarian missions could not have been any better.

The conviction in Pierre's stories gave credence to his belief in the role the veterans played in the world. Pierre served as an aeromedical evacuation technician in the U.S. Air Force. He explicitly spoke of the two consecutive days of rain, earthquakes, avalanches, tidal wave, and volcano eruptions in southern Chile in May 1960. He was deployed to Santiago during a humanitarian relief mission along with Canadian military forces. The vivid description of the two 400-bed, air transportable hospitals, the posted notices with instructions of the importance of getting medical attention to control the spread of disease, of treating patients, then shipping them to other areas within the country for more definitive care, had received the appreciation of the Chilean people. The value of the international cooperation and understanding has been a hallmark humanitarian deed called "the Amigos Airlift."

Pierre said, "In addition, to have had the privilege to be a part of the National Polio Foundation humanitarian mission in Akita, Japan, where approximately seven hundred polio cases were reported in August 1960, is indicative of how America partners with the world. The National Polio Foundation had provided assistance in Nairobi, Guatemala, Buenos Aires, and several sites in the United States with state-of-the-art medical equipment and vaccines to manage the polio epidemic for more than ten years prior to my deployment. Sharing medical science as a means of fighting or controlling polio in the world speaks volumes of the military capabilities around the world and not only as a peacekeeper."

In addition, I must share the widow's appreciation, affirmation, and respect for the U.S. Armed Forces and the military commitment to stand ready to assist the fellow human who cries for a Mayday, S.O.S., or any request for disaster aid in the world. Heidi is a German-born American who had been married to a retired U.S. Army Sergeant for 53 years prior to his death. Heidi's deep anger with those, who in her words have "the audacity of accusing Americans as the police of the world," was something idiotic for someone to say who had never had a desperate need for the assistance. "I do understand we cannot please everyone all the time, but for people in New Orleans, Louisiana, Homestead, Florida, or Biloxi, Mississippi, to say, 'I don't want military intervention in our business' during or after Hurricane Katrina, in 2005; Hurricane Andrew, in 1992; or Hurricane Camille, in 1969,' would be crazy. Despite the assistance of the Coast Guard, Air Force, National Guard, and other military entities, things were very hard for a lot of people during those days. My family and I lived around Keesler Air Force Base, in Biloxi, Mississippi, August 1969, and relocated to South Florida around Homestead Air Force Base after my spouse retired. Therefore, I can provide you with a first-hand account of the appreciation for military assistance. This is what I personally witnessed here in the United States."

Heidi goes on passionately sharing her stories of being a recipient of several humanitarian deeds as a child growing up in Germany after World War II. Heidi's emotional story of the Berlin Airlift, (known to West Berliners as "Air Bridge") describes West Berliners on the brink of post-war starvation after the Soviet Union closed all highways, railroads, and canals from West Germany into West Berlin in an effort to deny the people who lived there the food, fuel, electricity, and supplies required for survival, as well as any access to Western Europe. The United States and its Allies supplied the necessary cargo to West Berlin by air every day for over a year, until it was clear to the Soviet Union the blockade did not work. Heidi claimed those days are etched in her mind for life. She told another story of the "1954 Operation Kinderlift" which was the U.S. military providing a free four-week vacation to kids from West Germany to the German Federal Republic, via camps, group homes, and American families in private homes, and why she is so grateful for the U.S. military role in the world, even as she had the best spouse in the world for 53 years.

Heidi said, "I want more than anything, for the citizens of the world to realize America is not the police of the world, we are good neighbors who accept the responsibility of reaching out to help others in need." Heidi persisted I find a medium to tell her stories.

CHAPTER TEN

Greetings

"The veterans of our military services have put their
lives on the line to protect the freedoms that we enjoy.
They have dedicated their lives to their country and deserve
to be recognized for their commitment."

– JUDD GREGG, FORMER GOVERNOR AND
U.S. SENATOR OF NEW HAMPSHIRE

"Greetings," was an infamous life-changing word that many baby boomers, the children of World War II and the Korean Conflict era, feared to read. However, there were many young men during this period that accepted the word as a challenging opportunity in their lives as a positive option.

Mail from the Selective Service Board represented a draft notice or conscription for compulsory military service, starting with the word "Greetings." This effort had previously been employed a couple of other times, usually during a war period, but it was also used during the Cold War. It was re-established in September 1940 as Germany conquered

France and America supported the return of the draft. The word "Greetings," was followed with the words, "by the order of the President of the United States of America, Commander-in-Chief, you are ordered to report for induction into the Armed Forces." The addressee was given a date, place, and time to report for either a pre-induction physical or the induction physical with the written examination. Receiving this letter meant that the lives of most young men of the age eighteen to twenty-six would change forever.

Douglas retired after twenty-eight years of a remarkable military service, and his life was greatly affected by the draft. The courts had offered him a choice of six years in jail or volunteering for the draft. By law his military service obligation would have been two years of active military service and four years in the Inactive Reserves. Douglas said, "The draft was not an option I had considered or entertained during my adolescent years. The draft was not a popular word in 1967." As the strength of the military forces in Vietnam increased, more draftees were required for training and sent to fight in Vietnam.

Douglas acknowledged he grew up in one of the worst neighborhoods in Tampa, Florida. He saw the worst of the worst, both on the streets and in the low-income apartment building where he lived. But he was a good student in school, as well as a good athlete. Most of the older fellows in his neighborhood protected him. It was their responsibility to keep him away from the wrong crowd or other children doing the wrong things. Douglas explained how most of the kids who were perceived to be in the wrong crowd were now either dead or in jail. He claimed to always remember his grandmother's words, "A tree will always fall where it is leaning," in other words, "Be aware of where the people you associate with are going," and his grandmother would say, "Boy! Show me your friends and I will tell you where you are going." He said, "Grandmother's words live on forever in my life. I was an impressionable young man then.

"The words of my grandmother echoed in my head when I was arrested after winning the district high school basketball championship game. On my way home from the game after my so-called friends insisted I ride home with them, they told me to sit in the back seat, as they entered the gas station to get some drinks. Unknown to me, my friends took all kinds of things out of the store and did not pay for them. The two friends rushed back into the vehicle after leaving the store. I was somewhat confused and perhaps oblivious to what was going on around me. My two friends never explained what had happened in the store or the reason the driver was driving like a madman to get out of the parking lot. The manager called the police and reported he was held up at gunpoint, describing the vehicle and the two young men who had committed the crime. The manager had truly dramatized the robbery: He claimed the robbers had a gun only to get the police to treat the crime urgently. Before I was able to get a drink of my O.J. and find out why my friends were in such a hurry, police cars surrounded us and my friend Anthony was ready to make a run for it. But I pleaded and explained how nothing good would come from trying to outrun the police. The last word was hardly out of my mouth when the police car pulled up next to the vehicle driven by my friend and the tires on our driver's side were shot out. The car was out of control, and in what had seemed like hours to me, I saw my life flash in front of me. The next thing I knew, a policeman dragged me out of the vehicle with his weapon in hand and all the other policemen were aiming weapons at us.

The police were physically and mentally abusive, because the all-points bulletin went out with the manager's accusation that he had been held up at gunpoint."

During the police interrogation, the officers kept going on and on about a small sidearm weapon. Douglas claimed he did not have a clue what they were talking about. No one was able to locate the weapon allegedly used during the robbery in or around the vehicle. The police claimed each one of us had told them the other one had the gun. Douglas was sure that neither of the other two friends would have said he had the weapon during the robbery. This unfair tactic came after the police officers had physically abused them during the search of each person for the so-called weapon, which was nowhere to be found. Charlie and Anthony, the other two passengers in the vehicle, tried to explain to the police officers that Douglas had no idea what had happened at the gas station, but they wanted no part of the conversation. Douglas said, "It was obvious to me the officers had convicted us of a crime we did not commit without physical evidence and I was going to jail."

Two weeks prior to this ordeal, the basketball coach of the University of North Carolina had visited Douglas at his home, offering him and his mother and grandmother a trip to the campus as a potential basketball player. This was after several other universities had made offers, including the University of Miami and other schools up north. Douglas said, "My heart started racing real fast when one of the police officers explained being guilty of the crime by association, even if I did not go into the store with the weapon in hand. The officer said, 'Boy! You are looking at a twenty-plus year sentence in the correctional system. Once you go into that system, it is like a revolving door, you keep going back. But if you would only tell us who had the weapon and what they have done with it, the courts would be a lot more lenient on you.' During all these accusations when we were stopped or at the police station, at no point of the interrogation were we offered legal counsel," said Douglas.

During the robbery, Douglas was innocent and oblivious of his friends' intent as he sat in the car's back seat, replaying the tape of the game in his head. He said he saw that night's game in slow motion, including everything the coach had drawn up on the board, and at the same time really needing a cold drink. As usual, his friends always tried to protect him, so he believed this is why they insisted on him waiting in the car. He also knew several college and university scouts were in attendance during the game and hoped he showed them what they were looking for and more. He had always prided himself on being a team player who tries to make the right decisions right. He claimed how useless it was to simply do the right things, and that not doing the right things right is counter-productive. Douglas became very emotional as he explained how he had let his family down, made the wrong choice, and let the school, coaches, and community down, especially his grandmother, as her words kept echoing in his head. "You are defined by the company you keep."

He sat in jail day after day, week after week, because the bail was so high due to the gun charges, and Douglas' family could not afford it. He said, "This quiet time allowed me a true reflection on the consequences of my poor decision, naïve vulnerabilities, and how trusting I had been." The reality of it all was that his mother Daisy, a single parent, his grandmother, and two sisters, along with an older brother who was incarcerated at the Florida State Prison in Raiford, were in no position to assist him. His mother had been having a hard time making ends meet and could not afford to get him out of jail. He was assigned a public defender, who was overworked and underpaid. Things did not look too good for him as he sat in jail with lots of time to question himself. "Why me? How did this happen to me? I could have, should have, gone home on the bus, as I heard my grandmother's words over and over in my head."

A week before his trial, a high-powered attorney showed up to visit with him. He started asking questions and told him he would work with him as a pro-bono case. The word on the street was that this attorney was a friend of a friend of one of the coach's former players. The attorney was able to get the service station manager to admit he did not actually see a weapon and perhaps no one had physically showed him a weapon or had one on their person during the robbery. The station manager insisted Douglas was driving the getaway vehicle because the vehicle left the parking lot too quickly after they ran outside. The attorney was able to argue Douglas' case independently and did not involve his friends. Douglas could not explain how the attorney was able to work the deals he had worked out with the state attorney's office. The police officers never produced the alleged weapon reported during the robbery, and those charges were dropped. Douglas trusted his attorney with his life with one great concern, not to join his brother in the correctional system merry-go-round. He claimed to have felt blessed by watching and listening to all kinds of people speak on his behalf during the court hearing. The judge explained how it takes two people to have a child, but this community spoke very loud of this young man's character; therefore, he would offer him one of two choices. Six years in prison or two years in the military, which meant he had to volunteer for the draft. The next day he was on his way to Jacksonville, Florida, to the Armed Forces Examination Station (Induction Center) to volunteer.

Douglas was shipped to Fort Jackson in Columbia, South Carolina, where he underwent nine weeks of basic combat training. He graduated number two in his class, followed by eight weeks' advanced individual training as a company clerk at Fort Lewis, Washington, number one in his class. His drill sergeant explained to him all the opportunities for promotion with great reenlistment bonuses, though his chance to do so would be much better as an infantry rifleman. Douglas volunteered to go to jump school at Fort Benning, Georgia, for an additional three weeks. After completing jump school and finally getting to his first permanent station, he was promoted to specialist fourth class with only six months in the Army.

Students, pacifists, clergy, civil rights, and feminist organizations supported the draft resistance. There were draft card burning and protests everywhere. There were several doubts about the morality of the war and the Selective Service political agenda. However, the U.S. troop strength in Vietnam continued to increase, with more and more casualties, without a clear threat to the U.S. The need for non-commissioned officers had become greater. Therefore, the U.S. Army developed what was known at the time as a "shake and bake" with Non-commissioned Officer Preparatory School graduates becoming Sergeants (E-5). Douglas applied, was selected to attend, and graduated with honors. In between all the schools and working on his GED, Douglas played basketball on the post team. The senior non-commissioned officers and officers on the post admired his athletic skills. Douglas stayed humble as he always remembered his commitment to God while he sat in jail hearing his grandmother's words in his head over and over. He said, "I am convinced life is a treasure, nothing is guaranteed, as tomorrow is not promised. I only live God's plan each day, it is not about me and God's plan is greater than I could ever imagine."

Playing basketball was Douglas' safe haven, something he lived with as if it could end any day, but most people admired and respected his game as well as him being a very humble man. The Post Commander ensured he had the tools, so Douglas had everything he needed. He received the reenlistment bonus, coupled with the opportunity to entertain the troops, getting paid as he went from post to post or being on temporary duty, playing on the all-star team around the country, then getting back and being paid for each day he was playing ball, along with his monthly pay. He hoped never to go back to those low-income apartments in Florida.

Douglas' Post Commander reminded him of two famous draftees who served in the U.S. Army, Elvis Presley and Willie Mays, but they did not reenlist. The commander had overlooked Joe Louis, Sugar Ray Robinson, and Jackie Robinson. He said, "It was somewhat concerning to me, because these men were my grandmother's heroes. My grandmother had so many stories about Joe Louis ('the Brown Bomber'), Sugar Ray Robinson, and Jackie Robinson. She told me that Sugar Ray Robinson and Joe Louis were placed into the Army's Special Service Division rather than into combat and they traveled around performing boxing exhibition fights before millions of soldiers. Sugar Ray got into big trouble when he refused to fight exhibition fights when he was told black American soldiers were not allowed to watch the fights. During their travel they would experience blatant racism. Simple things, like being told to sit in the seats in the back of the bus on post. They were arrested by the military police because they did not move from the front. Joe Louis went to Jackie Robinson's aid, punching a captain who had called Jackie a 'nigger.' President Ronald Reagan said, 'Joe Louis was more than a sports legend—his career was an indictment of racial bigotry and a source of pride for both white and black people around the world.' Joe Louis was known during his war days for saying things like, 'We are going to do our part and win because we are on God's side; lots of things are wrong with America but Hitler isn't going to fix them.' Louis received full military honors during his burial at Arlington National Cemetery and it is my grandmother's wish that I will someday be buried at Arlington National Cemetery."

Douglas reenlisted several times, mentored several soldiers to illustrious careers, and made a difference in the U.S. Army, achieving a Sergeant Major—a rank only one percent of the enlisted force is capable of achieving in a career. He obtained his GED, bachelor's, and a master's in business administration. Douglas truly kept the world safe for democracy as he served in Korea and Schofield Barracks, Hawaii; then on his way to Vietnam he was rerouted to Japan. He also served in Panama, Italy, Desert Storm, and a couple of tours to Germany in his illustrious twenty-eight years of service in the Army—as a draftee.

Douglas was very grateful to the military for all the opportunities he was afforded, including his supervisors, mentors, teammates, and commanders who believed in him, but especially his grandmother, whose words had been his guiding light throughout his career. He was also very grateful to the judge who afforded him this precious journey in life.

But Douglas was very disappointed with the promise he understood the Department of Veterans Affairs had offered—"to serve those who have served." The demands of his occupation, being an airborne soldier, playing sports for years at all levels, and not reporting injuries while continuing to play ball or staying on jump status, meant he had several unreported injuries. It took Veterans Affairs more than twenty months before they acknowledged some of his medical conditions as service connected, but not his back condition, or his secondary leg issues, or hearing loss as a result of his occupation. The educational process or how to ascertain a veteran's entitled benefits should not be a treasured secret, as it appears to most veterans. Especially when it takes approximately twenty months at best before an applicant would receive their entitled benefit. Often veterans either give up or die before receipt of such benefits.

Douglas did not give up his battle for the benefits he was entitled to. He was denied service connection for his prostate cancer in his last rating decision. Since he had not served in Vietnam, the decision was that he was not exposed to the herbicide Agent Orange. It appeared to Douglas the VA staff may have tunnel vision when it comes to the words Agent Orange; therefore, applying the wrong rating schedule or legal standard to the rating decision. He said, "Records showed I served in Korea from May 1969 until July 1970. I believe the law grants presumption of service connection if a veteran served in the demilitarized zone (DMZ) from April 1968 to July 29, 1969. It would be more likely than not I was exposed to Agent Orange. I was assigned to the unit and have some stories to tell about some of the dumb things we did during my tour, like playing or staying on jump status while nursing an injury. I also know a retired full bird colonel that was a lieutenant during our basketball days in Korea, and he could write a buddy statement to reinforce my claims. I do have medical evidence that shows I had prostate cancer and all the secondary conditions. There are several sad things about this new battle. It is going to take another year or more, the burden of proof is on my shoulders, instead of the VA representative being trained to review all options before the denial of the award." Douglas made it clear, he did not want any handouts or anything he was not entitled to, but expected the VA to stand true to their word and serve us who have served.

Several years after our last meeting, Douglas' spouse Elaine contacted me, validating the trust and confidence she and her spouse had shared during our meetings. She explained how Douglas had been battling all his illnesses, secondary to the prostate cancer, as well as the VA bureaucracies. Elaine claimed he wanted me to know that the VA finally acknowledged after all these years, that his service in Korea at the DMZ during the stipulated period entitled him to the presumptive exposure to Agent Orange. The diabetes had gotten the best of him. He was deemed legally blind and received dialysis three times a week, along with several other medical conditions, and giving it all the best fight within him. Elaine said, "Miguel, I could not be any prouder of the attitude he has demonstrated every day. He often reminds me of our blessing and explained he wants his pilgrimage in life to be shared with society as a teaching moment. In the front of his files in the file cabinet is your full name, phone number, and a note in bold black letters saying, 'please contact the VA man, Miguel, in the event of my death and he will assist you with the death benefits arrangements.'"

Seven months after that phone call, I received the call Douglas directed his spouse to make. He had died of renal failure and his wishes were to be cremated and buried at Arlington National Cemetery. Elaine wishes to be buried with her spouse. The necessary burial benefit arrangements were made to include the Dependency and Indemnity Compensation for Elaine to receive her monthly benefits.

CHAPTER ELEVEN

My Companion Died,
So Why Are You Here Now?

> "I came here today to ask that this nation with all
> its resources and compassion not let my epitaph read
> 'he died of red tape.'"
>
> – ROGER LYON, IN HIS AIDS TESTIMONY BEFORE CONGRESS

O ne of the hardest tasks to manage personally or professionally as a field examiner and investigator in the Department of Veterans Affairs, Fiduciary Unit, was to knock on a door or ring someone's doorbell when the beneficiary had died before my arrival. Going to visit Ron was perhaps the worst of them all. I often recall witnessing the anger on the faces of family members as a result of their disappointment with the VA claim-processing requirements. The hostile behavior of Ron's companion, when I identified myself, was understandable.

Ron's first cousin, Janet, claimed to have been smitten with who this hero was, what he meant to his family, and the difference he made in the lives of many in society as a veteran and citizen. She described their family roots as deeply patriotic. Ron's father and three uncles were WWII veterans, his older brother a Vietnam-era Marine, and his sister had served in the Peace Corps in India. Ron's grandparents immigrated to the United States from Norway. They instilled core values of character, the importance of family, and making a difference as an American with much humor. Janet recalled how Ron worked every summer at the YMCA, as an adolescent boys' and girls' counselor. She explained how it takes a village to raise a child, but a real man to show them the difference. His expectation was to live up to his grandfather's legacy with humor as his tool of choice. Because Ron's grandparents would often say, "jokes open the widow of our subconscious," he readily established a vocabulary of his own, using malapropisms like "destruction" instead of "instruction," "ornamental" for "oriental," and many others adopted throughout the family.

The girls loved him and he appeared to love them; most of his friends were ladies. Janet was Ron's best friend and he confided in her about everything. It was understood, nothing in the world would come between them, as she described their relationship as unconditional love. While most of the family was sad, angry, and disappointed with the timing of this visit or the service rendered by the VA, Janet accepted the visit as an opportunity to share Ron's legacy. She strongly believed his life story needed to live on and requested permission to be present during the next revisit with the veteran's companion, Tim.

With a great sense of pride in the look on her face and the tone of her voice, Janet explained how Ron had found a niche as a photographer with a great eye for capturing the essence. At the age of 22, he was engaged to his high school sweetheart, Susan. But then he received that mail most young men of his age group were afraid of receiving, "Greetings, by order of the President of the United States of America you are hereby ordered to report for induction…" This was just two weeks after the engagement party, filled with laughter and talk of a family of his own. Ron perceived the draft notice as an opportunity to continue the proud legacy of his family. Serving in the defense of this country, standing guard, fighting to keep the wars off the shores of the United States of America, and the world safe for democracy, was how he took comfort with the notice. Knowing Ron well, Janet eloquently put it in words, "With a war going on, he couldn't not have been in the Army, and been a part of it." Somehow he soon had orders to report to Vietnam. Before leaving for his tour of duty in Vietnam, he returned home for thirty days and had a bigger party than his engagement party. Janet recalled how close he and his father appeared to have been, as they made laughter a part of the evening.

Janet had a box full of letters, pictures, cards, and notes—all the things that defined their treasured moments. Amongst them she read a letter he had written during his tour in Vietnam. He described how clever Charlie (the Vietnamese) were with the traps they set up to kill the soldiers and psychologically leave a lasting impact on those who discover the bodies. They would cover a deep pit with leaves and branches, which was then filled with sharply pointed bamboo sticks. To discover a comrade fallen into the pit is terrifying. He also described the trip wire that would catch someone's foot and trip an explosive or the loop that would pull the person up into the air when they stepped on it. For some reason she was compelled to share his last letter and explained her premonition or instinct that something was wrong or was going to happen. In his final correspondence while he was still in Vietnam, he explicitly described seeing other soldiers blown apart or impaled, terribly injured, or killed. He tried to cover up his fears and insecurities with humor or justify their misfortune as a learning opportunity by stating, "It will never happen to me because I am very wise to the threat, cautious, and very aware of each step I take." Three or four days after receiving his correspondence, his family got the notice of Ron being seriously injured in the field. He was medevaced for more definitive care and was stabilized for shipment back to one of the Army medical centers in the United States.

Letterman Army Medical Center, located on the Presidio of San Francisco, California, was Ron's home for more than eight months while he underwent medical treatment. It was the best of the best with a rich and impeccable history. Words cannot describe the quality of care and compassionate service of the staff, Janet said, explaining her perception when she visited. The legacy of the medical center went back to those soldiers returning from the Spanish-American War in the Philippines and during WWII. Its focus was on orthopedic medicine and rehabilitation therapy. This history was displayed on the walls in the lobbies around the facility, Janet explained. Rehabilitation therapy was required for injuries he suffered to his arm, leg, face, and a chest full of wounds from the explosive device he stepped on during the patrol in Vietnam. It was in his best interest to continue care at Letterman.

It was there that Ron was transformed from Ron to Ramona with a great affection for the gay community. The friendships he had established in the gay community, the freedom and culture in San Francisco, all convinced him he could not be married to a woman. Therefore, he broke off the engagement with his high school sweetheart, claiming he was not the man he was when they had agreed to marry. The gay community unconditionally accepted him with his disabilities, allowed him to love from within and to appreciate sex as lovemaking; an experience he had never known existed. Janet said, on many occasions he described the thrill and feelings, not realizing before those first couple of gay relationships was what lovemaking was all about. The freedom of being free in his world was amazing and ridiculous at the same time. When Ron was Ramona, she could out-dress any woman, with stunning make-up and clothing. Both men and women would compliment her for her glamorous, classy, sophisticated look. "If I did not know the real person, I too would have been confused," said Janet.

After playing and having the best time of his life, he started noticing some strange things going on with his health. This was later diagnosed as AIDS, although at that time, the condition did not have an official name. Janet recalled attending a medical conference, hearing of this new condition and how deadly it was. Her cousin had the textbook symptoms described at the conference and his prognosis was not good. He was very adamant the AIDS came from some blood he received after returning from Vietnam. He developed a deep sense of bitterness towards the Army and government for his failing health and would not accept the responsibility for causing it.

Ron's significant other, caretaker, and business partner, Tim, had a lot to share on their disappointment and perceived reason for anger with the bureaucratic system in the government. The emotional passion in his voice as he questioned my untimely visit after his Ramona's death was very clear and loud. Neither was he short in expressing his disappointment with the service to the veterans. I walked up to the house and rang the doorbell. When there was no answer I went back to my government vehicle and was about to write a note, explaining the need or importance of seeing the veteran. Then the limousines showed up from the burial service and his hostile behavior, after I identified the purpose of my visit, was understandable. The questions, "My companion, my cousin, my brother, my son, my friend has died, so why are you here now?" asked by most in front of the home, on that Tuesday afternoon, were some of the hardest questions I had ever had to answer.

I truly appreciated the fact that Janet accepted the reasonable approach to the situation and managed the understandable anger, disappointment, and sorrow with what she claimed her cousin would have preferred, dignity and class. I extended my apology and condolences on the behalf of the government. I shared with them that arranging their busy schedule was greatly appreciated, and in the best interest of the family. I did not perceive or treat this as just another case and monthly quota. Instead I requested another meeting because the veteran did not live long enough to receive the more than $100,000 entitled retroactive pay before he died. Ron passed on before my visit; therefore, the money could be deemed, "escheat to the state" which meant funds could go to the state as unclaimed funds on an absence of legal claimants. Therefore, it was my moral obligation to assist or advise the family on how they could legally obtain some of the funds or most of the money with receipts for care or service rendered. It was hard to disregard the family's needs over the consequences of being reprimanded for making an unofficial visit back to a known decedent's residence. I arranged my schedule and allotted ample time to share my wisdom, knowledge, and understanding on the legal way for the family to ascertain the veteran's entitled benefits. The privilege of the family and his companion sharing the veteran's life story with me was very therapeutic for them.

Tim was still grieving over the passing of the love of his life and masked it with an outburst of emotional anger. He explained how it should not have gotten to this point. He had tears in his eyes and blew his nose while he attempted to speak of the weekly calls to the VA Regional Office with negative results. He described how angry and sad it made him, when the person on the other end of the phone told him, "Because of the privacy act and patient confidentiality, I cannot talk with you." Tim said, Ramona only had months to live and he tried to share this information with the person on the other end of the 1-800 number and they would tell him the same thing—"The privacy act does not allow me to talk with you." Tim explained, "Before things got real bad, Ramona would get on the phone, provide the required information needed for the privacy act, then render the authority to allow me to share information needed on the case." But as Ramona's condition worsened, growing anger and disappointment with the government bureaucratic system would get the best of her, and she just refused to get on the phone during the last months of her life. It saddened Tim to no end: Watching and caring for the person he loved more than life, while Ramona was so ridiculously consumed with the feelings or thoughts that the government ruined her life. Tim said, "I agreed with Ramona, she was drafted, sent to Vietnam to fight a war, stupidly stepped on a trap, got injured, and was sent to one of the most fabulous Army medical centers. She then somehow contracted AIDS. She died without a total confirmation as to how or when she was infected with the virus. Ramona always admitted having unprotected sex while she was a patient and liberated. But she was also given blood during the medevac out of the war zone and perhaps while she was at Letterman."

The U.S. Army medical community was emphatic in their communication to Ramona about their airtight clinical protocol on blood management during the last twenty-eight years. It was clear in their statement; the veteran was not infected with the virus while at Letterman. In the healthcare community, Letterman Army Medical Center is world-renowned for its great accomplishment with the research in the artificial blood science. But Ramona died believing that somehow, some way, she was infected at Letterman, despite the promiscuity during that period in her life. Ramona would always start singing the 1969 anti-Vietnam song "War," sung by Edwin Starr, popular on all the radio stations of the time. She sang the lyrics over and over, Tim said, as a way to console herself. She would sing it as her anthem. Because after singing this song over and over, she would say, "War can take lives or kill dreams but I will never allow it to take my life or kill my dream." This is why she tried so hard with a personal conviction not to allow her injuries to define who she was or what she was in society.

After Ron's discharge from the U.S. Army, he was awarded an 80 percent service-connected compensation for his disabilities. Three years later, that was reduced to 10 percent service-connected compensation because he failed to show up for a scheduled physical examination or reply to the VA letters directing him to report for the examination. In an effort not to allow his disabilities to define who he was, Ron had relocated and embarked on the refurbishing of homes known in San Francisco as "the painted ladies," old ornate

Victorian homes. Therefore, he did not receive the correspondence from the VA Regional Office and the medical community. Ron was so focused on the crazy money the new refurbishing business was bringing in, that he simply disregarded the reduction in his VA monthly income. In his mind the government had found out he was making crazy money and reduced his income. The Social Security Administration found out because the IRS had reported the money he paid in taxes. He had to refund Social Security for the extra money he had received from his business, exceeding his allowable amount. So Ron had those reasons to believe the VA had reduced his benefits and was waiting on the day when they would contact him to refund the extra money. He also had a very successful food business in Mexico. During that period in his life, money was no object. Money only led him to more promiscuity and drugs.

Tim described Ramona's trips to Mexico and Canada as therapeutic for medical treatments, obtaining medications and drugs that she could not obtain in the United States. In the last two years of Ramona's life when her condition was worsening, making those trips was not easy and the treatments were not as effective as they had been. Despite Ramona's conviction to not allow the government to control her life or dictate who she was, she contacted the County Veterans' Service Office for assistance in filing for service connection for AIDS/HIV. Ramona was totally convinced she was infected with the virus while she was still on active duty. But after hundreds of dollars for world-renowned, credible, medical opinions describing the state or interpretation of her blood when she was discharged from the U.S. Army, it was more likely than not, she may have a trace of the virus. Tim could not, or would not, explain any further detail on this matter. He only said, "I submitted the documents to the County Veterans' Service Officer and requested to reopen a claim to be reinstated for those service-connected conditions Ramona had been reduced to. She did not receive the future scheduled physical examination or the reduction VA notification letters. Due process is by law a must, and Ramona was denied her rights because the letters were sent to the wrong address. The VA medical community had the correct address and so did the finance center, but the systems do not speak to each other. Tim had a legal power of attorney, but the federal government did not recognize it. Tim called these bureaucratic processes "obstacles that prevent a veteran from obtaining their entitled benefits before they pass on." It is not a customer-focused system that takes the extra step to provide service, but instead is solely driven by the numbers.

Answering Ron's survivors' hard question, "My companion, my brother, my cousin died, so why are you here now?" in such an environment was not the best moment for information-sharing in the best interest for anyone. During most visits, after establishing mutual trust and respect, often veterans, their families, or survivors are eager to share their life stories or their legacy with others. I had to reschedule a second unofficial visit to educate Tim and Janet of the options available. I explained the reason I was sitting in the government vehicle and writing the note was to inform Ron that the reason for meeting was to release the awarded funds. I also told them I had made several telephone calls with negative results prior to the visit. In desperation, I contacted the release of information section at the VA medical center for the correct address, and then made that embarrassing, humiliating trip, so I could release the funds. I acknowledged how words could not express my sincere condolences to the family, friends, and companion or the embarrassment, sadness, or disappointment with the agency's bureaucratic system. The need to meet the Regional Office's imposed monthly quota was irrelevant to doing the right things right, which was arranging the subsequent meeting. That visit was a win/win for everyone.

Ron's cousin, Janet, extended her appreciation of being included in the meeting to share the reason why she had been smitten with who and what Ron meant to her, or society, for that matter. He was a master of female behavior, which was developed as a child, surrounding himself with females, understanding who they were, and why and how they do the things they do. This is why his transformation to a female was so natural. She remembered taking him to his medical appointments, seeing the look of admiration from most of the people in the waiting room, both men and women. When the receptionist or medical technician would call his name, and "she" would acknowledge it by standing, the looks on their faces or reactions to the moment were priceless. Janet's unconditional love, respect, and admiration for her cousin were very clear. She concluded after talking about all things she had said, "Ron was very funny, loved by those who knew him, and he allowed those around him who accepted him for who he was, to fully enjoy their time with him."

Tim was totally consumed with emotions—the sadness, anger, and joy for having had the privilege of knowing and being allowed to share the life of a person he loved more than life, he would often say. He was also appreciative to be allowed to speak about his Ramona's stubbornness, defiance, or headstrong ways in not allowing society to define who she was or what she should be. "In some ways, it made her successful," Tim said. "In others, twice as hard to become a reality, because she refused to allow her disabilities to infringe on what needs to be done. Her constant thoughts of her parents' and siblings' disappointment in her drove her harder to be more than anyone expected. She was proud of being who she was and her accomplishments." In between Tim's tears of anger, remorse, or appreciation, he offered his deep sentiments and story freely.

The most gratifying opportunities for me were the privilege of actively listening to the stories, being trusted by the family, and being able to confer with my trusted Senior Veteran Services Representative, who mentored me through it all with his encyclopedic knowledge. He was my authorizer back in the day, and he provided me with the correct applicable procedures or processes with the statutory laws, the applicable requirements, and how to obtain a customer-focused, idiot-proof list for the survivors to legally attempt to obtain the pending withheld funds.

Ron had been supporting his mother after the death of his father, providing more than fifty percent of her support. Actually, he was paying a hundred percent of her support and declared her his dependent. Ron's estate was able to continue the support of his elderly mother.

CHAPTER TWELVE

The POW Widow Has a Son and Granddaughter Deployed

"To honor our national promise to our veterans, we must continue to improve services for our men and women in uniform today and provide long overdue benefits for the veterans and military retirees who have already served."

– FORMER U. S. REPRESENTATIVE SOLOMON ORTIZ

The initial assessment of this widow was mindboggling. Why would such a strong woman who has so much going on in her world be deemed incompetent? She demonstrated an amazing capability and exceptional ability to balance family affairs with her health issues, but minor issues could overwhelm her.

She is an example of a veteran's spouse and mother who never learned or adapted to the modern, "politically correct" way of life. Dorothy told it like it was, and marched to her own drummer. She lived every day for her family with the remarkable memories of her spouse Tom's (whom she called "Daddy"), prisoner of war (POW) journey and nightmares.

Her description of living with Tom and listening to days of captivity in the Korean POW camp for the last 57 years was emotional. She said, "Daddy fought in the Korean War, survived those brutal days in the POW camp, and had to fight the VA for his entitled benefits until his death." It was clear the thought of his battles angered Dorothy to no end. The challenges of raising three children and then two grandchildren later in life during her son's deployments, working from home (as an accountant), and managing some local small business accounts, had taken a toll on her. This was in addition to the greater challenge of caring for a PTSD-disabled POW veteran with a serious pride idiosyncrasy, who was a deep thinker and could be charismatic one day or introverted the next day.

The widow's distrust for the VA's inabilities was noted with several of her comments. In particular, the one in regards to the benefits department's lack of urgency in providing service to the veterans in a timely manner. She said, "Daddy could not comprehend how a nation like the United States of America can put a man on the moon, can put satellites into space that can read the time on a Russian's wristwatch, but cannot develop a better system to process and manage veteran's claims. Too many of Daddy's friends gave up filing for their disabilities or died before receiving those benefits," she said, with tears in her eyes. She explained how Tom received a home loan and the G.I. Bill for education as soon as he got out of the military. The first thing was his GED and then a training program to become a meat cutter. Securing a job after the Korean conflict on the heels of World War II was very hard. There were too many WWII veterans still trying to get on with their lives.

Tom had lied about his age; he was only 16 years old

when he volunteered for the draft. He was in Korea fighting the war at the age of 17, when he was captured. There were a couple more 17-year-old American soldiers and Marines in the same POW camp as he. When Tom first applied for his service-connected compensation benefits, he was told his enlistment was fraudulent because he lied about his age; therefore, he was not entitled to compensation.

Tom had grown up to be, despite the repeated brutal torturing by Chinese Communist Guards in the Korean POW camps, a very proud man to have served and survived the war. He strongly believed it was his moral commitment to this nation to fight for freedom. Things were hard on him during that time in his life. Dorothy said, "Daddy loved this country and what it stood for in the world, despite the brainwashing techniques they were subjected to, which convinced several American captive prisoners to refuse repatriation. They chose to voluntarily live in the Republic of China. The thought of accepting handouts was incomprehensible to him, and, "if the VA denied him service-connected disabilities because he actually lied about his age to fight a war in defense of world peace, then that is the way it is." Tom never submitted another application for VA benefits for years. He was happy to come home alive with all his body parts to see the lady he had promised to marry when he got back.

Tom's older sister, Jackie, was Dorothy's best friend. He was three years younger than they were, without a cause and not much ambition in life. Jackie and Dorothy were getting all dressed up at Tom's house on their way to the junior/senior prom, and Tom only 14 at the time, said, "I will marry you when I grow up: You are the prettiest girl in the world." Dorothy said, "I was a cheerleader for the football team and my boyfriend was one of the star players and if he found out what Tom was saying, it would not be pretty. I told Tom never to say that again because I had a boyfriend. I was his sister's best friend and our friendship meant too much to us. He was too young for me and should find someone his own age." He did not like school, so when a couple of his older friends volunteered for the draft into the U.S. Army, going along was an easy choice, pretending to be 18 when he was actually 16. He left for basic training along with the others and a couple of months later he came home, looking real good, unbelievably mature. He was on his way to the war in Korea. His parents invited a couple of friends—including Dorothy—and some family over for dinner. Dorothy said, "For some reason Tom insisted on taking me home after dinner; I obliged and we had a memorable evening. He told me he would marry me when he got back from the war."

Tom wrote home, telling about his long journey over to Korea, and all the people he met or some of the crazy things they had done. At first, someone would hear from Tom at least once a week, then a little longer after a couple months in the war zone. He would explain how bitterly cold it was and tell of the terrible conditions. He said, "I can't talk about what we are doing, but someday I will tell you more." Then the letters stopped and no one heard from him or knew of his whereabouts for months. His parents contacted everyone they could think of, and finally one day his parents received a letter from the Department of the Army, stating in part, "Tom is missing in action in Korea. The enemy forces attacked Tom's company position, forcing it to withdraw. Unofficial information received by the Department of the Army indicates your son is a prisoner of war; however, its authenticity cannot be verified until the International Red Cross can officially validate Tom as a prisoner of war." His parents always believed he was alive, because no one had ever brought his body home to them, and they said, "Tom was too ornery to die. Ornery people ride off into the sunset." It was almost two years before the Red Cross acknowledged and notified the family of his captivity. Dorothy claimed not to be as optimistic as his parents, life moves on and so did she. She kept a copy of his letter amongst her precious memorabilia from Tom for years.

Dorothy was in her third year of college, working for a law firm and dating a hot-shot attorney who was self-centered, not a man she would have enjoyed marrying and having children with. He later became the District Attorney. Dorothy said; "I had such strong feelings for Tom and could not commit to marrying anyone else until I validated my true feelings for him. The wonderful time I shared with Tom the night before he left for the war lived on."

Jackie called her with the excitement of Tom's discharge from the Army upon the completion of his medical examination and debriefing at the port of embarkation hospital. Dorothy said, "I had many dreams of the first time I'd see Tom again, if I would see him again, and all kinds of wonderful thoughts of us. Waiting for him to get home was forever. I had so much to say and not sure how to start. In the back of my head he was my best friend's little brother." Tom came home months after the war was over and everyone was excited to see him. "It was embarrassing to me because the only person he kept asking for was me," said Dorothy. His parents had gone out to welcome him home at Letterman Army Hospital in San Francisco, and he kept asking about Dorothy. As luck would have it, Dorothy had final exams the day he arrived and was unable to see him right away.

She said, "When I saw him, my world ended, it was all

about him. During the years I realize my initial feelings for Daddy, was a motherly instinct. I wanted to take care of him, be the mother of his children, and be his everything. He told me, the main reason he maintained his sanity and overcame the brainwashing tactics or torture was because he lived in the future with me. Whatever was going on in his life, he would see her in that prom dress, changing into her wedding dress to marry him, the faces of the people as they walked down the aisle, their honeymoon, making love, the birth of each of their children, and those thoughts enabled him to overcome any pain and take up a lot of time in solitary confinement. The game he played in his head was, yesterday is gone, today is a bad dream, and tomorrow will be the day I wake up from the bad dream, which was his release date, known as 'Operation Big Switch' when the captives were exchanged. That is how he survived each day because the mind is such a powerful thing with love as the reason, nothing else in the world matters."

Tom and Dorothy got married six months after he returned home. He was able to purchase a home under the G.I. Bill as a wedding gift to the love of his life. Dorothy said, "Daddy would always say he 'loved me more than life itself. Life is to love me. You are my purpose for living every day.' He did not only say these words, he lived them every day of our life." They have three children, two daughters and a son. The oldest daughter, Christina, is a nurse manager of the operating room; the second daughter, Carol, is a bank manager, whom we appointed as the fiduciary payee for her mother. Both daughters were very attentive to their mother's needs and proud of the love their parents instilled in them. Their only son is a deputy sheriff and an Army National Guardsman who has been deployed four times to either Iraq or

Afghanistan and was now back in Afghanistan. Divorced for the last 15 years with four children, two of his children were living at home with his mother. Dorothy's oldest grandson is a career U.S. Army Non-Commissioned Officer and a granddaughter is a U.S. Marine, also deployed to Afghanistan.

Christina and Carol described their mother as a lifelong caretaker who had sacrificed both education and career to care for their father when he came back from the Korean War without a high school diploma. Christina said, "My father was very demanding and uncompromising about his children's education and for them to become productive members of society. Without an education, but with a dream and love for my mother, he was hired as an entry-level employee to cut and process meat in the local grocery store. Attending butcher school in the evenings after work, he received a certificate in meat cutting. Battling with his war demons, PTSD, and depression, Daddy enrolled and received an associate degree in meat processing and food safety. Daddy became the regional director responsible for inspecting beef, lamb, pork, poultry, and seafood, as well as the proper use of hand tools and power equipment for such tasks as slaughtering, chilling, aging, and cutting, as well as food safety and sanitation, marketing, and customer service. He spent a lot of time on the road, but got us up early in the morning to check our homework and would always remind us of the privilege of being free, a lesson he learned as a captive POW. He told us over and over, how the Chinese government mobilized hundreds of young volunteers to work in the POW camps to brainwash the prisoners. Another POW who chose to live in China had said: 'My family and millions of other Negroes and I, have suffered under the brutal attacks of white supremacy and the cruel slave laws of the southern states. This suppressed me from being who I am or could ever be. I need to try another way of life where I may have a chance of being deemed a working-class citizen.' This is what weak-minded people do with the lack of self-confidence in desperate times."

The sisters simultaneously agreed Daddy's point was, "We must believe in self. If we don't believe in ourselves, then why should anyone else believe in us? We will overcome. Trusting oneself is our greatest investment in life." It was amazing to watch and listen to each of them finish one another's statements in regards to their father's life lessons and acknowledgement of wisdom. The two of them wondered whether Daddy really understood their high-tech math homework, but he diligently got up early in the mornings to review it along with all the other schoolwork they were doing. Later in life as "we reminisce of those days, we would laugh, but we recognized our father only wanted to emphasize the importance of homework and this was his way of doing it."

Dorothy said, "Daddy was like a stubborn mule. He didn't apply for his entitled VA benefits for years, always saying, 'There are others who need the money more than we do. We make good money and have the best family insurance.' It was his belief VA funds were like welfare money. As a child of the Great Depression, he vowed never to be a recipient of welfare funds or a menace to society. I believe this is why he never pursued VA compensation benefits. It was not until several people he respected convinced him to join the Veterans of Foreign Wars (VFW) organization. Daddy joined, explained what he was told years prior about his enlistment being fraudulent, claiming to be eighteen when he was only sixteen. It was almost 18 years since his discharge and the VFW had assisted with the processing of hundreds of similar cases with positive results, which made Daddy very happy. A year later,

September 1973, almost 19 years since his discharge, Daddy received a letter informing him of the fire at the National Personnel Records Center, in St. Louis, Missouri, and that the VA could not continue to process his claim. These letters came from the VA for years, explaining why they could not grant the service-connected conditions, because there were no service records to validate the issues. It angered Daddy to believe this great nation would be this incompetent and treat their veterans and former POWs with such disrespect, especially when he got back from a compensation and pension physical examination. He claimed they treated him as if he was a criminal, and not forthcoming with the truth. The VFW did not give up, and somehow after several years, Daddy was granted 50 percent service-connected compensation. Daddy never explained to us all the intricacies of what the VFW had done to achieve the 50 percent disability for him; they convinced him that the funds he received were entitled benefits and not welfare money."

Christina, a registered nurse with a master's in nursing, said, "Daddy's frustrations had just begun. My parents were very grateful and comfortable with the fact they were receiving VA funds, which were not a handout. They accepted these funds for years as they were intended, as compensation for conditions that were caused during his military service. These conditions worsened with age and secondary conditions manifested requiring medical care. Daddy would visit his board-certified family doctor, who would diagnose a disease, secondary to one of the VA's granted twelve service-connected conditions. Months later, Daddy would be scheduled for a compensation and pension examination with a physician's assistant or a nurse practitioner to evaluate the disease and render a medical opinion. The redundancy is terrible, especially for a veteran with serious mental issues. What makes it worse is waiting another six-plus months and the VA provider disagreeing with the board-certified doctor's opinion. It took Daddy back to the brutal torture he endured in the POW camp by the Chinese Communist Guards. The appeals process takes another four to five years and people of Daddy's age often do not live to receive it. For example, Daddy was hung upside down by his legs, from beams, hoping he would talk and provide the guards with information needed. He was made to stand for days without being allowed to move, and beaten with clubs and rifle butts. His board-certified neurologist provided a thorough neurological evaluation, showing a sciatic nerve condition, which was likely caused during his military service, but the VA physician's assistant denied any service connection. Five years later the Board of Appeals granted service connection, secondary to the lower lumbar spine condition. This was the other battle Daddy endured the last years of his life."

Carol for some reason felt the need to apologize for not being as medically versed as her sister, but expressed her sincere commitment in assisting her mother in having the best quality of life possible. Carol said, "Mother has been the glue that kept our family together and it is going to be hard limiting her involvement. Mother's baby, our brother Tommy, Jr., still resides with her, along with his two children. It gives Mother a reason to get out of bed every day. During Daddy's last years it was amazing how he constantly thanked her for being the woman, spouse, mother, and best friend he dreamed about while in captivity and claimed he would not have made it without her love in his life.

"Tommy, Jr. and the VFW arranged Daddy's burial and home-going at the National Cemetery. Tommy emotionally encapsulated our father's legacy, as a journey of a hero, from the forgotten war where many younger men died so we could live in a free world. The words of so many people, telling of the difference Daddy made in their lives; the unbelievable stories told of the brutal torture during captivity shared by Daddy with so many people as a way for them to appreciate freedom, coupled with *Taps* played by a soldier at the graveside and the 21-gun salute, assured there was not a dry eye in the crowd. Mother was very proud of her choices and sacrifices. She married her best friend's younger brother, had their children, and trusted his love for her would afford them the pleasure throughout their 57 years together. During the ceremony, Mother hugged the flag presented to her as tears streamed down her cheeks. She said her final goodbye to Daddy as his body was laid to rest. Mother said, 'I don't have words to express this moment of my late spouse, Tom; I'm sure he's proud, very humbled by the service today. He was very brave during his last journey. He was alert to the last and I will live forever with the memories of our deep crazy love. I believed in his love and we trusted our love for each other.'"

Occasionally I visit with veterans and their spouses addressing sensitive topics, and feel as though I am walking on eggshells. Since her family doctor had deemed Dorothy was having some problems managing her finances and recommended she have assistance, the VA appointed a fiduciary payee to assist her. She had put aside her education to put her family first, managing her family's household and living the life of a POW spouse, mother, and grandmother, so I had the challenge of ensuring her dignity while delivering a sensitive message of having assistance with her financial affairs.

Dorothy's children, grandchildren, and the community rallied around and partnered with her without compromising her pride and devotion to the things that were valuable to her. Tom's legacy continues with his son and grandchildren serving in the armed forces, standing guard and keeping the world free for democracy.

CHAPTER THIRTEEN

The Dream of a Female Pilot in the U.S. Army Air Corps

"Congress should stop treating veterans like they're asking
for a hand out when it comes to the benefits they were
promised, and they should realize that, were it not for these
veterans, there would be nothing to hand out."

– FORMER U. S. CONGRESSMAN AND
REPRESENTATIVE NICK LAMPSON

The dream of a little girl—to fly a United States military aircraft in support of the world's freedom—was considered to be insanity during Sharon's childhood. She would share her love of having the ability to fly and touch the sky with anyone who would listen. She shared the journey of her trials and tribulations during this unforgettable visit. This day in particular is etched in my mind forever.

Those of us who were living in Florida during the hurricane season of 2004 can remember those days vividly. We experienced four named hurricanes to bash Florida in a six-week period: Charley, Frances, Ivan, and Jeanne. I was directed by management to continue with the appointments and conduct the scheduled field examinations. It was all about the number of cases completed, with no regard to the inconvenience of the beneficiaries or anything else. The human part—living conditions, road safety, or anything other than conducting a field examination—were irrelevant. The monthly quota was the bottom line and the most important thing toward my supervisor's bonus. I recall making the appointment to visit this family first, because the widow, Alice, lived in the same zip code as my next call and Alice was under terminal hospice care.

Trying to find Alice's residence was quite a challenge as a result of the aftermath of the hurricane. The landmarks and road signs to her address were gone, as well as some homes were missing and roads flooded as a part of the hurricane destruction. I was a half-hour late and the thought of this visit still nags me today. I knocked on the door, Alice's daughter answered, and when I identified myself, she said, "My mother is having a bad day today, but we need to make this happen, because we have been waiting too long—twenty-two months—and we need the money to pay the bills we owe." The bills were sitting on the living room table at the front door.

Just after we finished with the administrative part and she signed the VA forms agreeing to be the Veterans Affairs fiduciary payee, the hospice nurse urged us to come see Alice immediately. We hurried in, Sharon took her mother's hand, and as her mother squeezed it, we watched Alice take her last breath.

It instantly took me back to July 4, 1970, in Tuy Hoa, Republic of Vietnam, when I witnessed my comrade Ruby get hit and take his last breath next to me in the bunker. Composing myself to maintain my professionalism in the presence of the family and the healthcare providers was very difficult, but I persevered. I immediately contacted my supervisor at the Regional Office and informed him of Alice's untimely death. Alice died minutes after her daughter signed the fiduciary agreement appointing her as the legal custodian to manage her mother's financial affairs. I suggested we not process the report of death immediately until the pending funds were released which was a sizeable amount. He said, "Hell no, I will never be a part of data integrity compromise," and verbally admonished me for suggesting such an action. I described the family's financial dilemma with an explanation of the family's commitments, especially since they had been expecting to receive these funds for the past twenty-two months. "It was no fault of theirs," I said, that Veterans Affairs had taken so long to process the beneficiary's claim and for the widow to die while I was visiting her. My supervisor said, "Miguel, I have told you once and I will tell you again, 'hell no', and I will not talk about this again. We have done our part and are not responsible for what is going on in the adjudication section of the Benefits Department. We will be credited for our visit and that is our only concern at this point." I expressed my disappointment with what I had perceived to be an unreasonable position or unwillingness to be creative in entertaining another opportunity to serve our beneficiary. Instead, I was summoned back to the Regional Office for a reprimand for behavior unbecoming. The American Federation of Government Employees (AFGE) Union and I fought the reprimand until it was removed by the Director of the Regional Office. I was not privileged to the outcome of the entitled funds for Alice's expenses or whether the family had to wait to receive the accrued funds or final payment.

Leaving the now-deceased widow's home and sitting in

the government vehicle, a couple of blocks away from her residence, and staring at the storm's destruction, I found myself weeping uncontrollably. I had never allowed myself to internalize my responsibility to serve those who have served, or their dependents. I finally continued on, facing all the hazards on the roads after the worst hurricane to hit Florida in twelve years, including bridges out, live electrical wires, poles and trees down, and with road signs missing. Many homes were without electrical power and families were displaced. They were distressed and I was trying to maintain my professionalism in representing the Department of Veterans Affairs with quality and class. I finally made a decision to cancel my appointments and reschedule them for another day. I contacted the assisted-living facility where the next beneficiary resided, to attempt to reschedule, only to find out Sharon (a former military pilot) wanted no part of rescheduling her appointment. The veteran's son, Kevin, came on the phone and said, "My mother does not believe in leaving for tomorrow what we can do today, we have an appointment and we will keep it." I wondered, what else could go wrong after my first appointment? Fortunately, the other two scheduled appointments agreed the conditions on the roads were too hazardous for a visit and one of the families did not have electrical power.

I was also late for Sharon's appointment after wandering around and making several calls to the assisted-living facility owner for better directions to her location. Roads were either flooded or closed as a result of fallen trees or poles blocking the passage. At that moment, my thoughts were, "I don't need this, and there must be a hidden message someplace or something greater than me forcing this visit; because emotionally I felt weak and not in control of my faculties to effectively manage the meeting." But Sharon had challenged me not to leave for tomorrow what has to be done today. More importantly, meeting and listening to her journey in life was worth the risk of facing those hazards that day after Frances had caused significant hurricane damage to the area.

This is a day that I must admit impacted my life and I am so grateful to Sharon's demand that I keep the appointment. I rang the doorbell of this well-maintained, ten-bed assisted-living facility in an affluent neighborhood. The owner announced my arrival to Sharon and her son, Kevin, who were sitting on the dock out back, having a cigarette. Sharon seemed somewhat confused and said, "You don't look like a Miguel, can I see your government identification?" I asked her, "What does a Miguel look like? She said, "Not like you." I replied, "I could say the same about you. I was expecting to meet a more senior-looking person whose birth date is from 1922. That would make you over 88 years old, but you don't look it." Sharon was 5'4", weighed 111 pounds, and had beautiful hazel eyes and well-kept short red hair, with a little splash of gray. She had been a U.S. Army Air Corps pilot and very much a lady. She lived her life exemplifying those qualities, but it appeared to me she had issues with trust and being in control. After the morning I had already experienced, feeling hopeless and thinking I had failed that veteran's family, being summoned back to the regional office to meet with management, coupled with the episode of uncontrollable emotions I experienced sitting in the vehicle, it was a challenge for me to move forward.

Recognizing these concerns and how imperative it is to create an environment conducive to information-sharing, I shared my story. I had been a black officer in the Air Force as a healthcare administrator specializing in medical logistics. Recalling some information in the documentation I had received from the Regional Office, indicating Sharon had been an officer in the U.S. Army Air Corps, I had to establish our commonality, and having been an officer as well could not have been a better fit. It appeared as if someone had turned on a bright light in the room when Sharon began to establish a sense of trust in who we were, a kindred moment. She said, "You were a black officer and I was an aviator-woman who happened to be an officer in a man's world—the good old boys' club during those days. You were from the Panama Canal Zone and I from a little town in Iowa." The revelation of both of us having been officers was the beginning of Sharon's trust and comfort level in sharing her childhood dreams and intriguing life journey.

The astonished look on her son Kevin's face spoke volumes to how amazed he was to see his mother's eagerness to share her story. He knew his mother had been deemed incompetent for VA purposes as a result of her struggling with memory issues in recent years; this was even before I defined my purpose or reason for the Veterans Affairs visit, to ascertain the required information to validate her medical condition. The initial perception of Sharon's need to be in control of her environment was very obvious at this moment. I remember vividly as if it was yesterday, her saying, "Young man, I was the second daughter with two brothers and me in the middle of those rascals, then a baby sister who always wanted to be the baby, in a town in Iowa that was only about five and half square miles wide with lots of water. I went off to war with an expectation of living my dream, flying military aircraft, but ended up in California, across the bay from San Francisco, as a certified public accountant. Growing up, life was a never-ending battle. To maneuver though each day,

I had to be strong, and my father insisted we kids were. I lived his words every day, 'a weak mind is a weak soul and a weak soul is non-productive.'" She talked about the way her brothers challenged her as a young lady to be their equals. They were fanatically obsessed with flying. Sharon could not be any other way, but to be a student of the aviation program. They were intrigued to learn about the Wright brothers, and how they could not have done that first flight without their sister Katharine's assistance. Sharon's brothers would build hang gliders for flights and she would have to go up in them because she was the lightest, but they all crashed. This is why they believed Orville and Wilbur Wright may have done the same thing. Later her older brother went off to flight school, learned how to fly, then came back home and shared his knowledge with them. She claimed to be a much better pilot than her youngest brother who was only eleven months younger, nearly the same age.

America was at war and both of her brothers answered their call to go fight for their country as U.S. Army Air Corps pilots. Then in 1942, President Roosevelt requested the establishment of the Air Transportation Auxiliary. He based this new initiative on the English female pilots who ferried planes throughout the British Isles. Sharon got word that the Army Air Corps had an increased need for pilots with experience and would consider females to fly aircraft on non-combat missions. It would be a way to get her foot in the door. She volunteered and applied, along with thousands of other women, with only 2,000 accepted and 1,074 graduated. Sharon was assigned as a civilian to the Women's Auxiliary Ferrying Squadron of the Women Airforce Service Pilots (WASPs). Her assumption, to receive equal pay, pension and disability benefits, overseas pay, government life insurance, and death benefits as granted to the Regular Army aviators, was false. It did not apply to the auxiliary units. The women were treated worse than the black pilots in the Air Corps, just because they were women. She said, "I will not say those black pilots were not treated horribly. This is truly an example of what the glass ceiling was all about. We could see the top, but women were unable to break through the glass ceiling standing on a cracked floor without leverage" She asked if I understood why women had to be as strong as blacks in society. "The more things change the more they remain the same," she said.

In World War I, female civilians working overseas with the Army had served without benefits. A congresswoman in Massachusetts had introduced a bill that if women served in a war theater they would receive the same benefits as the Army male officers. Somehow by World War II not much had changed. When she delivered a plane to England and went to the Officers' Pilot Club, they told her women were not allowed. The commander stood up and explained, "This woman is not just an officer; she is a lady with the rights as any aviator and gentleman in this club." She was allowed to stay and was served as a lady.

The Women's Army Auxiliary Corps' benefits had not changed much. It was remarkable how Sharon appeared to remember things so clearly in the course of our meeting. Especially when she said, "A bill was passed in 1959 granting WAACs who had chosen not to continue serving to be credited with active duty credit. This is why it took my son so long to get my entitled Veterans Affairs benefits." Medical documentation to validate Sharon's medical conditions that had occurred either while she was serving or aggravated by the service was nowhere to be found.

Sharon said, "I was no different than most aviators about their medical conditions. We were/are somewhat guarded and we often self-medicated to stay on flying status. I had some urinary tract problems, thyroid disease, bad allergies—especially in some parts of England, high blood pressure, which was under control with medication from the medics, and back problems, for which I sought medical assistance. The VA said, no record of any of these conditions were available; therefore, I did not have these conditions."

Sharon's late spouse served during WWII, which entitled her to be granted a VA pension after numerous denials for her own service-connected disabilities. It was a stop-gap measure to assist with the bills. Her son never gave up. He wrote lots of letters to the Department of Veterans Affairs and finally contacted the Defense Advisory Committee on Women in the Services, who are concerned with the status and benefits for women who had served. Sharon was finally able to receive VA benefits in her own name, instead of in the name of her late spouse. While Sharon related this chain of events to me, she visibly displayed her anger and disappointment with the disparity of male and female pilots.

Sharon said, "I had to leave the job I loved as much as life. Being up in the skies amongst the clouds, my wings touching the sky, had been my childhood dream as it was my brothers', along with having a family. But, it was clear women who became pregnant would be immediately discharged, back in those days. I did not want much; only to serve my country, fall in love, and have a home with a family like a career military person. In 1943, a year before the program was disbanded, I gave up flying and started a family. I have two sons, six grandchildren and fourteen great-grands, a true blessing. I have the best son anyone could ask for, my Kevin. I would not have had it any other way."

The privilege of hearing the lifelong journey of this pioneer woman first-hand is truly an experience I am honored to share. It was disappointing to acknowledge the risks Sharon endured in her life in the defense of the world freedom. She was forced to abandon her dream so she could have a family, only to be denied her entitled benefits, unlike her brothers who were able to live their dreams of flying and have their families. This dedicated woman bravely supported the war as a result of the shortage of male pilots, and then fought for female equality and against the VA bureaucracy in vain.

Unfortunately, Sharon died prior to the final adjudication of her case.

CHAPTER FOURTEEN

He Volunteered for the Draft as a Way Out

"As we express our gratitude, we must never forget
that the highest appreciation is not to utter words,
but to live by them."

– President John F. Kennedy

Unknown to most of us, the politics of the draft moved beyond the shores of the U.S. into places like the Republic of Panama.

A childhood friend of my uncle in La Boca, Panama Canal Zone, shared his twenty-one year journey in the U.S. Army and how his life-changing opportunity came about. Leonard was a U.S. Army veteran who had volunteered for the draft during the Korean Conflict, known as the Unforgettable War. He served two tours in Korea and two tours in Vietnam as an Airborne Ranger. Serving several other assignments in the U.S. and overseas, as a proud "guardian of world freedom and a professional military educator whom others emulate," was something he spoke of with heart-wrenching pride.

Leonard had volunteered for the draft with several oth-er young men, sons of the men who had migrated to Pan-ama City, Panama, from the West Indies or the Caribbean to build the Panama Canal. The French attempted to build the canal through Panama to join the Atlantic Ocean with the Pacific Ocean—but failed, after nine years and the loss of about 20,000 lives in the attempt. Many West Indian laborers were employed with other workers from the French islands of Martinique and Guadeloupe. It was concluded that they lacked resistance to the mosquitoes carrying malaria, yel-low fever, and other tropical diseases. A solution, nearly a medical miracle, came through Dr. Col. William C. Gorgas. He assumed the herculean responsibility of managing the sanitation system and disease prevention of yellow fever and malaria, transmitted by mosquitoes in the Canal Zone. Because of his work, it was more than eighteen years before another yellow fever death occurred in the Canal Zone.

That he was an educator was evident when Leonard deemed the need to provide a lesson on world history from the 1950s. He said, "A very surprising political approach to world affairs occurred when the United Nations condemned the June 25, 1950, North Korean invasion of South Korea. The U.S. and the Soviet Union divided the Korean peninsula into north and south. The U.S. imperialists saw the southern half of Korea and the puppet regime they installed there as a major element in their plans to contain and perhaps wage war against the Soviet Union. It was after the People's Republic of China was founded that the U.S. saw that a pro-U.S. govern-ment in South Korea was crucial to surrounding, contain-ing, and threatening the spread of communism in Asia. The People's Republic of China was only a year old when it was directly threatened by the United States with the outbreak of the Korean War. President Harry Truman authorized forces into Korea with other member nations under U.S. command. President Truman's administration directed the Governor of the Canal Zone and Consulate of Panama to offer the President of Panama, José Remón Cantera, an opportunity to be a part of controlling communists with troops of young men who were born in the Canal Zone. These young men were born under the United States flag in Gorgas or Coco Solo hospitals and deemed eligible for the draft. Leonard described this agreement as a very calculated political move. Most of the young men in question were of West Indies or Caribbean descent (Jamaica, Barbados, Trinidad/Tobago, Montserrat, Martinique, etc.). Descendants who lived in what were classed as the silver cities of the Canal Zone were targeted as candidates for the draft. He explained how the one hundred square miles of land surrounding the Panama Canal were deemed as the Canal Zone and divided into two classes, silver cities and golden cities. Therefore, for every one of the young men from one of the silver cities, mostly considered black, it was one less young man of the golden cities, mostly white, required for the draft in the Canal Zone. Each of the U.S. territories had draft quotas and the Panama Canal Zone was required to fill their quota.

When Leonard graduated from high school in 1951, he was self-employed as a tailor, and his father was not too pleased with his son's decisions. Leonard was the first high-school graduate in his family, but had no true definitive direction or vision in his life. He described that point as being blank, as he was unsure of his future. It was rumored in the silver city communities that there were outstanding opportunities for those who volunteered for the draft. They would have unlimited benefits, see the world, get a free advance education, and have healthcare for life, to name a few.

Leonard went to Fort Amador, a U.S. Army post in the Canal Zone, and inquired about the rumored opportunities. The information he received was so enticing, that he volunteered for the draft and sat for the entrance examination and induction physical in February 1952. He scored very well on the written examination. Leonard was very athletic; therefore, he passed the physical examination like "a walk in the park." He acknowledged his accomplishment with pride as the beginning of several challenges he was proud of achieving and willing to talk about.

The troop ship was not scheduled until April 1952, so he and 29 other recruits had to wait for shipment to basic training. When the ship finally arrived at Cristóbal, Panama Canal Zone Port, the recruits were all transported on a bus from Fort Amador to the Atlantic side of the Isthmus of Panama for transit to the United States. These young men were leaving home for the first time. They were headed to an unknown place in the world, perhaps a war zone, filled with uncomfortable feelings of the uncertainty. The recruits had never been on such a large ship and were not sure what to expect. Leonard explained how sick most of the recruits got, while conditions worsened on high seas. The nine-day journey to the United States seemed much longer.

The ship made stops at Puerto Rico and the Virgin Islands to pick up more recruits on their way to basic training. "We finally docked in Brooklyn, New York, for disembarkation," Leonard said. Upon arriving into New York from Panama in early April, Leonard described the temperature as extremely cold. However, he quickly acknowledged the weather in New York was in no way close to the cold weather he was forced to endure during the Korean Conflict.

The recruits were transported to the reception center at Camp Kilmer, New Jersey, for assignment. Leonard and several other recruits were sent to Fort Campbell, Kentucky, for their eight weeks of basic combat training, followed by eight more weeks of advanced individual training as an infantry soldier, airborne qualified. He was promoted to the rank of Specialist Fourth Class upon completion. Leonard explained how an airborne-qualified soldier, during those days, received $55.00, which was half a month's pay, for jumping out of a perfectly good aircraft and was respected by all. He remained with the 11th Airborne Division until they were shipped to Korea. Leonard described his second journey on a troop ship to Korea, as one of the greatest tortures any human being could endure. He and everyone else around him were seasick as a result of the worst weather of the year at sea. The thought of going to war when he arrived in Korea and having been so seasick is something he would never forget. He finally got to Korea, feeling weak from the long journey with all the unexpected emotions he experienced, but the bitter, inexplicable cold weather was most memorable. He described it as bone-chilling weather, and even wearing multilayered clothing could not minimize the cold. He recalled asking himself, "How do people live in a place like this?"

The great fear of never leaving the peninsula of Korea alive was very strong and real in his mind. The decision to volunteer for the draft and leave wonderful warm Panama, for a place like Korea, was beyond stupid or justifiable. He prayed and made a promise to himself, "I, Leonard, will leave this God-forsaken place a better man than I was when I arrived." An iron-willed young man, who lived up to his word, he said, "I got there as a young man and left as a mature man with a solid outlook on life."

Many feared this was the first step in a communist campaign to take over the world, and nonintervention of the Panamanian government in collaboration with the United States was not an option. He explained how this presumption was based on philosophical belief. The communist campaign will take over the world, and must be stopped in this God-forsaken place. It was well understood that "the fight on the peninsula of Korea was a global struggle between the East and the West or good and evil. At my age now, I do believe it was in my best interest to be a part of making a difference in the world," Leonard said. He sat in his favorite recliner and talked about the fight against the Koreans, Communist China, and even the weather as one of the toughest enemies in that brutal war. He strongly believed no one could really describe the historical struggle. The inhuman choice of first having to kill a fellow man or be killed, then going on to the next firefight while trying to survive the weather was a battle within the war. The weather in Korea was either extremely cold or very hot, he admitted with a smile. He said, "Another very memorable thing about Korea was the pungent scent of kimchi in the air. Kimchi is a popular Korean dish known around the world as highly seasoned and marinated vegetables that ferment with a strong, lasting scent. It seemed when the weather was hot the scent subsided." These memorable events, the weather, and the aromas were experienced at the young age of nineteen. He has lived these events over and over ever since then. He recalled how his greatest fear was of not having fear.

Life goes on and so do we. All the military training he received prior to going to Korea could not prepare him for such an act of survival and how to deal with some of the biggest rats in the world. He had to develop the elements of trust, dependability, reliability, visualization, and self-confidence to survive in that world. Leonard goes on to describe the experience as one of the key factors enabling him to be a much better person with appreciation for the finer things in life and a more sensitive man in society. Today and throughout his successful military career he employed these great elements of life as core values.

Enduring the war in Korea gave him the confidence he would be able to achieve anything in life, if he truly believed he could. It was the platform he stood on for the rest of his military career, especially after his assignment to the 3rd Division at Fort Benning, Georgia, in 1954. Being a Hispanic black was another type of struggle he encountered as he fought for acceptance. He described himself as a very good athlete, who started playing sports as a way of communicating who he was. His master plan and talents allowed him to be accepted and respected as a member of the post team.

Leonard volunteered for a reassignment into the Airborne Unit he always admired as a child growing up in La Boca, Panama Canal Zone. He was selected to serve with them. Being assigned to the 193rd Infantry Brigade, Fort Kobbe, Panama Canal Zone, was like an unbelievable dream. As a kid, Leonard observed these soldiers playing baseball and other sports with incredible teamwork, which he admired. Even the parties after each game appeared to be such an exciting example of the true spirit of sports with fun. The Brigade exhibited their commitment to fitness by the daily 0530 hours four-mile runs. It appeared to be a one-for-all, and all-for-one family unit. Leonard always had the greatest love and respect for those soldiers he saw doing the things he admired and now he was living the legacy, an unthinkable dream.

He met his childhood sweetheart who had two of their five children in the same hospital where he had been born. Gloria truly represented "the hardest job in the military is the role of spouse." Leonard said, "Gloria has been the glue that kept the family together, my career and family life had been seamless because of the person she is. She acted like father and mother during my frequent absences, in addition to managing her thirty-five-year career. Every time I was reassigned to another post she had to start over in another environment. This is why I kept leaving and returning to the drill sergeant at Fort Dix to minimize the changes. I left home at 0300 hours and returned after the kids were in bed around 2130 hours, or served overseas fighting a war and defending the freedom of the world.

Gloria said, "I had to take the kids to all their games and they played every sport available. In the military as your spouse gets promoted his spouse is expected to take a more active role in the other spouse's support and Leonard was promoted every time he was eligible. My family was first. We had to have our family day on Sundays. After church we had brunch at the non-commissioned officers' club. As the kids got older, they would take care of each other, the older takes care of the younger ones." "The confidence and trust she garnered in the family were the key factors in enabling me to be the best of the best in everything I faced," said Leonard. "My teammates respected me, co-workers admired my dedication, and supervisors supported my devotion to the mission. No man is an island; next to him is a better person, his partner and spouse. None of my awards would be possible without her. I am blessed with the best of the best," as he held her hands and looked into her eyes with such passion his sincerity was apparent.

After three dream years in Panama and three other assignments which included a promotion to staff sergeant with training as a drill sergeant at Fort Carson, Colorado, and serving as a drill instructor, Leonard returned to Korea in 1964 as a peacekeeper. The spicy scent of kimchi was the first thing to greet him back to Korea. Not being there fighting a war, but playing war games, watching the Koreans watch us at the two-mile wide Demilitarized Zone was interesting, Leonard said. He could not wait to get back to the "world," the United States. Returning to Fort Dix, New Jersey, in 1965, he shared his wisdom of the Korean War as a drill sergeant for three years to soldiers who would later go to Vietnam.

Leonard and the Army deemed the need for a more modern war tactical approach. He was reassigned to Phu Vinh, Republic of Vietnam, in 1968 for a better appreciation of the conflict in Southeast Asia. It was reported that about 2,500 Americans were either killed or wounded during the Tet Offensive in Vietnam, a month before Leonard had arrived at another war zone. He still had problems facing death or having people around him die, even after the brutal fourteen months on the front line in the Korean Conflict. He explained how to look fear or danger in the eye, and no matter how hard the journey, they never left a comrade behind. The weather in Vietnam was almost the same as it was in the Panama Jungle Survival School. Training in Panama was textbook correct, as expected in Vietnam. He had some vicious firefights as a young man in Korea and learned a lot of combat tactics from those experiences. Being a Sergeant First Class and controlling those troops he trained had been his greatest challenge. His devotion to the military was not about him; it was for the men and women he could inspire and lead to make a difference in the world, he admitted with pride. The application of those life-surviving skills and tactics he trained the recruits on, during the three years as a drill sergeant, was something he found hard to adapt. The expectation of training did not equal the experience required in the world conflict. The U.S. troops fought a jungle war, mostly against the well-supplied Viet Cong, who set up attacks or ambushes with booby traps and escaped through complex underground tunnels. They would also hide in dense brush and thus the need to drop Agent Orange, which would clear an area for the troops. It was difficult to determine which, if any, villagers were friend or foe. Soldiers commonly became frustrated with the fighting conditions in Vietnam and the politics of the war. Many masked their frustration with drugs—an addiction many Vietnam veterans found as the only comfort after the harsh experience in the jungle of Vietnam and lack of acceptance upon returning home. This profound outcome was one of the psychological warfare seeds Communist China had planted in our society as a war tactic.

The wisdom and knowledge he obtained were great tools used to teach other drill sergeants how best to train the new recruits when he was reassigned back to Fort Dix, New Jersey, as a drill instructor again, in 1969. Two years later, Leonard was promoted to Master Sergeant and returned back to the Mekong Delta as an advisor. The war continued to become more political and frustrating. The military was saying one thing and politicians were saying something else. Members of the U.S. 1st Air Cavalry Division refused an assignment to go out on patrol by expressing "a desire not to go." This is one example in a series of American ground troops engaging in "combat refusal." The headquarters for the U.S. Army in Vietnam was decommissioned May 1972, but Leonard and other non-commissioned officers were not allowed to leave until July 1972. He was re-assigned to Fort Dix, New Jersey, as a First Sergeant until he retired.

Leonard described the honorable twenty-one years of military service during his retirement ceremony, as a blessing, a privilege for a poor kid from the Panama Canal Zone, who had no direction in life. This humble man of honor is the first to say, "Politics afforded me the opportunity to make a difference in the world, serving as a guardian of world freedom and a part of history. I used sports as a social bridge in establishing trust and unconditional respect. It was all about teamwork and appreciating each other."

Leonard's pride would not allow him to apply for his entitled Veterans Affairs benefits. He had served in the Korean Conflict and two tours in Vietnam. He had pushed recruits through basic training and admitted with pride of the couple hundred times in his ten years as a drill sergeant he graduated with his troops. He also jumped out of airplanes as an Airborne Ranger. He was always concerned about his rank or position in the military and perhaps, due to that part of his ego, he would ascertain hallway consults from the medical team in the unit, without formal documentation. Policy states that without documentation, no injuries occurred, and several of Leonard's service-connected disabling conditions are not addressed. Leonard repeatedly defined his position toward his service-connected disabilities as, "I have borne the brunt of the national wartime sacrifice for years in keeping the world safe for democracy, with honor, dignity, pride, and an expectation I would not have to fight for my inherited entitlement." It was, sadly, truly a false assumption on his part.

Leonard said, "Miguel, with all the little differences I may have been a part of in the world, I am equally proud of being a part of some of the soldiers who returned from the Korean War as postwar boomers wearing flip-flops. It was a cheap rubber edition of similar footwear we wore as youngsters growing up in Panama. It was made from a piece of automobile tire and an inner tube around the foot to keep it in place. Legend has it, the first flip-flops started to appear after World War II as soldiers brought Japanese zori back from the war, often as souvenirs. Japanese children have traditionally worn them when learning to walk. In society, flip-flops have become a defining example of an informal lifestyle and came to represent the California lifestyle in general and surf culture in particular. It seemed like all the kids wore them to the beach or the pool. To be a part of the evolution of the changes of the fashion landscape as much as athletic shoes, jeans, and t-shirts in our society today. Many kids wear flip-flops all the time, replacing their athletic shoe trainers. The workplace started relaxing, with experiments like casual Fridays and casual summer dress codes wearing flip-flops.

"These precious memories of where I came from, who I am and the difference I made in the world can never be denied or defined by the Department of Veterans Affairs with compensation or pension. There are veterans with greater needs for their benefits than I. Reflecting back, God has been good to me, I am blessed and favored."

CHAPTER FIFTEEN

Kodiak Coast Guard COMMSTA– the Land of the Midnight Sun

"Our veterans accepted the responsibility to defend America and uphold our values when duty called."
– U. S. REPRESENTATIVE BILL SHUSTER

"Who would believe the limitless opportunities in the Armed Forces, especially when we are speaking about the U.S. Coast Guard and a kid from 'L.A.,' that is, 'Lower Alabama?'" asked Jeff Johnson. He had retired after forty-four years of dedicated service to our nation in the U.S. Coast Guard and the U.S. Army. Jeff had lived in or visited six of the seven continents of the world, including serving in Vietnam, but he still marvels over "The Land of the Midnight Sun." This was a life he had experienced for three years with his brother, a fellow Coastie, and for five years as they planned a trip after retirement to relive the dream most young men never even realize. They took that road trip, riding their motorcycles from Mobile, on the Gulf Shores of Alabama, for 15,500 miles, according to his odometer, to Kodiak, Alaska, and stood on top of the world in the Arctic Circle.

For Jeff, the battle of adolescence in the late sixties in this country was nothing but a big, never-ending party, until he dropped out of college. He said, "I was in big trouble, my girlfriend was having our first child, no money, no education, and without an education deferment, a sure ticket to Vietnam. In 1969 the Vietnam War was transformed by a new policy called Vietnamization. The Tet Offensive, with more than four thousand Americans killed during that campaign, forced General William Westmoreland to call for an even greater commitment of combat troops in Vietnam, which had reached a half-million. He had believed it would bring victory inside three years. The U.S. forces were stretched around the globe and more troops were needed. It was obvious to me then, the war in Vietnam was going strong and my draft notice would be in the mail soon. Because the draft continued to exempt college students and skilled workers, critics increasingly denounced the conflict as a rich man's war but a poor man's fight. My best solution was to visit an Army recruiter and to be proactive, instead of reactive. I had to be in better control of what was the best for me. If I had to go to Vietnam, it would be to serve doing something I had a say in doing. Therefore, I enlisted into the Army and got married to afford my family a more responsible future than the big party we had been enjoying. The year in college paid off, as reflected in the great scores I received on the armed forces entrance examination. I had the pick of the litter in which military occupational skills (MOS) and career choices were available to me and I had chosen electronic aviation."

Jeff's twenty-seven-and-a-half-year journey of active military service began with a trip to Fort Benning, Georgia, for nine weeks of basic training, including the zero week processing. Jeff expressed his strong confirmation of the value, in lessons learned, during basic training. They contributed to the unwavering love for this country and the pride he had developed in serving with people of all walks of life. He believes it should be an obligatory experience in the life our adolescents.

Jeff was shipped directly to his arduous Airborne Radar Repair School, at Fort Hauchuca, Arizona, for seven-and-a-half months. There were twenty-six soldiers that started school, but only six graduated. Upon completion of the course they would maintain the sophisticated sensor equipment on the OV-1 Mohawk military aircraft. This aircraft was vital to the mission in Vietnam, which meant that 90 percent of the class had orders to Vietnam. The soldiers who washed out of the course were mostly made infantry soldiers on their way to front lines in Vietnam.

Jeff's aviation unit in Vietnam was seven miles outside of Tuy Hoa Air Base, the base where I was also stationed at the time. We started sharing stories and interestingly enough, one of his most memorable moments was the July 4, 1970, attack, when he was ordered to set up a bunker on the beach side of the compound. The bombs sounded closer and closer, so he dropped the sandbag, ran, and drove into another bunker, only to learn later a rocket had hit the sandbag he had been carrying. The Viet Cong had also launched an attack on our base, at which time I witnessed my comrade take his last breath. It was an interesting healing moment for us both, but Jeff peeled back deeper combat scars, which made my experience seem like a walk in the park. He described some things that have haunted him for years, in particular, a trip up to Cambodia after a massive campaign, with the enemy suffering large casualty counts. The U.S. soldiers had dug a large hole as a mass grave to bury the dead, but they had underestimated the required capacity, so the soldiers had to dismember body parts to accommodate the requirement and then go to breakfast afterwards. It appeared to be another day at the office.

President Richard Nixon authorized a series of bombing raids in Cambodia and sent both U.S. and Vietnamese Army troops across the border, all without the consent or even awareness of Congress. When the secret Cambodian campaign was revealed in a *New York Times* exposé, President Nixon announced, "We had no troops in Cambodia or Laos."

Jeff said, "Among all the atrocities I had witnessed, the one that lives on more than any other is the young girl who had crawled under the fence, strapped with bombs to blow up our aircraft. The lieutenant's orders were to capture her and not kill her. She avoided being captured, was able to blow up a couple of aircrafts on the flight line, and was later was shot to death. Now that I am retired, without distractions and time on my hands, the Vietnam War lives on a lot clearer in my head. I see this little girl and hear her voice with all those who were shooting at us and we shot back until they stopped shooting. I no longer have to suppress or hide those demons to stay on flying status and lead the troops without medical assistance.

"At the end of my tour in Vietnam, I was promoted to specialist (E-5), with a little over a year remaining on my enlistment and an assignment back to Fort Hauchuca. This time back, I was the Grumman OV-1 Mohawk Aircraft

Maintenance Trainer for the enlisted members, pilots, and operators of the aircraft until my Expiration Term of Service (ETS)."

After his discharge from the U.S. Army, Jeff relocated with his family to Georgia and sought employment with an Army National Guard Unit as a civil service technician. He found the traffic in Atlanta to be more than he needed or wanted to deal with. The Army National Guard unit where he was working was a state agency and not the federal government, as he had expected. Therefore, he resigned. He was a product of a military family, his grandfather served in WWI, along with his father and several other family members in WWII and Korea. It made him much more comfortable to inquire about opportunities with other branches of service. The U.S. Coast Guard recruiter gave all the right answers, in the best interests of both Jeff and his family. The recruiter appeared to be more appreciative of his skill set and made him an offer he found to be the best option. This included going up to Coast Guard COMMSTA, Kodiak, Alaska. He enlisted into the U.S. Coast Guard at a lower rank, a Petty Officer Third Class (E-4), which was one rank below his rank at the time of his discharge from the U.S. Army.

The recruiter had understated the role of the Coast Guard in the defense of this nation's security and the privilege of being stationed at the Coast Guard COMMSTA, Kodiak, Alaska. Jeff said, "Let me tell you, Miguel, the Coast Guard is a maritime, military, multi-mission service, unique among the U.S. military branches for having both a maritime law enforcement mission (with jurisdiction in both domestic and international waters) and a federal regulatory agency mission as part of its mission set. It operates under the U.S. Department of Homeland Security during peacetime, and can be transferred to the U.S. Department of the Navy by the President at any time or by the U.S. Congress during times of war. Its motto is *Semper Paratus* (Always Ready). As one of the country's five armed services, the Coast Guard has been involved in every war from 1790 up to the Iraq War and the war in Afghanistan. It is also a consolidation of five federal agencies: the Revenue Cutter Service, the Lighthouse Service, the Steamboat Inspection Service, the Bureau of Navigation, and the Lifesaving Service. We have dedicated everything, including our lives, to the proposition that the American Merchant Marine, carrying needed supplies to the far-flung battlefields, shall not be too late with too little. We might be a small branch of the U.S. military, but we have big responsibilities to protect our shores at home, often done quickly and quietly without much fanfare or any attention at all. The unfortunate but necessary thing of rescuing our citizens during national disasters, including the hurricanes, tornados, earthquakes, floods, and Mayday calls at sea, in addition to putting a stop to drug trafficking are not necessarily the perception we are most pleased with. The lasting images of a Guardsman rescuing people on rooftops during hurricanes and national disasters speaks to most people's perceptions. Controlling oil spills, setting up safe serving communication grids during our national disasters, and providing the world with real-time weather accounts are little quiet responsibilities we are a part of."

The Coast Guard COMMSTA, Kodiak, Alaska, was turned over to the Coast Guard in 1973 from the U. S. Navy, a couple of months prior to Jeff's enlistment into the Coast Guard. It is one of the largest operational bases in the Coast Guard and the largest in the Pacific area. The base operates and maintains HH-60 Jayhawk and HH-65 Dolphin helicopters and the HC-130 Hercules fixed-wing aircraft. The station's primary mission is aerial search and rescue in a large area of responsibility covering the Gulf of Alaska with the Pacific Coast, the Bering Sea, and the Bristol Bay. It is also responsible for patrolling offshore fisheries and deploying helicopters aboard High Endurance Cutters operating off Alaska. It provides logistical support to various Coast Guard units in the area, which also includes transporting aids to Navigation LORAN personnel who maintain a remote navigation station, only accessible by air.

Jeff said, "This was a golden opportunity for a newbie like me. I had to learn to adjust quickly and adapt to so much so fast, it was unreal. Aside from all those professional requirements, the opportunities to live with the midnight sun, Kodiak bears, unbelievable hunting and fishing, snowstorms lasting days, camping in true wilderness, motorcycling the Alaskan outback, and much more. In the long run, it all paid off. I was promoted as early as possible with greater responsibilities and enhanced management skills. The Coast Guard being so small, people are closer with each other and the word gets out on each guard's work ethics and ability to be a team player. Somehow people believed I could do much more than I imaged I was capable of doing.

"The initial introduction was to sea patrol duties, which can last three to six months away from families. At this point I realized what a tough job it is to be a 'Coastie' spouse—I believe it is the hardest job in the military. It is like Murphy's Law, nothing goes wrong around the house until we are out at sea and then the wheel falls off and it is all up to the spouse to take care of it or make it right. Being the financial manager, doing the plumbing, working the electrical issues, along with automobile repairs, any personal or health concerns, and so on. The spouse would also be the mother and father, which at times confuses the child when Daddy returns home. The spouse has to deal with all the special occasions, and the changes in the children's lives, including that day our young, innocent thirteen-year-old daughter, Melanie, walked out of her bedroom as a teenager. Her mother asked her to go back into the room and send our innocent daughter back out, because she could not believe she was our Melanie. This little girl, who claimed to be Melanie, had all the answers and we were too old to understand anything. She was a totally different person. My spouse needed the sweet, innocent twelve-year-old, Mother's girl who went into that bedroom the night before, not the brat of a child that showed up that morning in question. By the time I got back home, there were other issues we had to deal with and make clear with a father-to-daughter understanding. I missed a lot of special family events, which can never be replicated. Establishing rules and not being around to enforce them were one of my greater challenges and disappointments. The fear of the unknown with the limited communication opportunities for our dependents during deployments is so hard on us all.

"I have nagging thoughts about the year I allowed my then ten- and eight-year-old daughters to attend our next-door neighbor's burial service at the national cemetery with the Coast Guard community. For my eight-year-old, it was the start of her nightmares every time I was leaving on a trip, as she would see me coming back home and going into that hole. The story in the Coast Guard community was that our neighbor was killed in the line of duty, trying to apprehend a drug runner. Our oldest daughter Melanie never said a word about it, but would demonstrate such an appreciation when-ever I returned home from my trips. She kept those lasting feelings and memories within.

"The thoughts of us standing guard around the world to minimize the drug and contraband traffic into our country or illegal fishing on the high seas, with all those high-powered weapons the runners or fishermen are carrying are terrifying day-to-day ways of life for Coasties and their families. The family left at home often suppresses thoughts of the worst outcomes—these are the hidden stresses we share together as families, for the world.

"There was nothing else more clear from all the mandatory levels of professional military education courses we attended, than a leader leads by example and strength; a well-defined plan is to have the best possible outcome. So leaders bridge the gap between plans and outcomes. But to employ this clear education at home, I faced this rejoinder from our daughters: 'This is our home, not a military organization. I am not one of your troops who have to fall in line.' I suffer a constant battle due to those words, because we were trained to lead, not negotiate. I have to admit, the balancing act of family and service to this nation was very hard. During this period in my life, I was learning, adjusting, and doing the things to capitalize on the privileges I was afforded, being accepted and respected in my profession. Working harder instead of smarter was the only thing I knew best. These learned adjustments were the foundation and platform from which I stood on the journey of the illustrious career I had.

"You see, Miguel, to say the military had been good to me is an understatement. When we think of me quitting college at the end of my freshman year, getting married without an education, joining the military to provide for my upcoming family and the unknown, the military afforded me the opportunity to obtain a bachelor's and graduate degrees and to serve, live on, or visit six of the seven continents of the world. I learned to lead, to appreciate members of all walks of life, and to develop lifelong friendships, which included one of the most memorable trips I ever made—with a Coastie brother for life—to the Philippines. They called us a Salt and Pepper team. We made the journey of the heart-wrenching World War II Death March, of the Japanese POW camps.

"Our friendship will live on forever, appreciating the value of those Aleutian Islands the Japanese occupied, seventy years after seizing control of Attu and Kiska islands early in WWII. The U.S. and Canadian forces pushed them off of American territory. It is the shortest route between the U.S. and Japan, which lies through Alaska and out the Aleutians. Whoever controls the Aleutians has the whole control of the ocean without a constant threat to Alaska, Canada, and the U.S. The opportunity to serve as a Private in the Army, and be able to retire as a Chief Warrant Officer in the Coast Guard and make a significant difference in the world was great. These privileges are not without personal sacrifices. Spending sixteen of the twenty-seven-and-a-half years in the service overseas, serving in Vietnam, working at long-range navigation LORAN stations with fourteen years in the Pacific and two years in the Mediterranean, yet I was a divorcé, without the opportunity to be a solid part of my two daughters' upbringing as I would have preferred. After ten years as a bachelor, I had the privilege of meeting and marrying the best companion any man could dream of having. This marriage has been for the last twenty-five years. The Coast Guard provided me with the best marketable skills, which afforded me the opportunity to continue supporting this nation as a civil servant with the Coast Guard for seventeen more years.

Accepting Jeff's declaration of his illustrious career and

the pride he expressed in his chosen profession, the limit-less opportunities afforded and joy he experienced as a Guardsman are accomplishments beyond my imagination. I believe most other military members or most Americans are oblivious of these things. Sitting across from him with admi-ration of his journey and achievements, I reflected on my own limited knowledge of the Coast Guard. The incorrect perceptions of the role of the Coast Guard, held by many, are amazing. I recalled the veteran I visited who said to me, "The Air Force and Coast Guard were like the Girl Scouts of the Armed Forces."

My neighbor Bob's father, Gerard, is a proud member of the Veterans of Underage Military Service (VUMS), and had served in every branch of the military service, except the Coast Guard. In their retirement years of telling stories and a bit of military one-upmanship, and because Gerard's brother was a retired Senior Chief Petty Officer Guardsman, Gerard would often goad him by saying, "The Coast Guard is noth-ing but fresh-water sailors, river rats, and puddle hoppers, not real warriors. I served with real warriors in the company G-187th Airborne Unit in Korea at the age of seventeen, with my good friend, Rudy Hernandez, who is the last living His-panic American Medal of Honor Korean War recipient. This is what real warriors do: We fight to defend this country's interest. We do not just ride around in boats policing the beaches, checking the girls, and arresting those drug runners or rescue people out of the puddle."

Bob said, "My dad had done everything to convince me not to enlist into the Marines or the Coast Guard. Dad would say, "I know best, I enlisted into the U.S. Navy when I was sixteen years old with my friends who were eighteen and nineteen in Massachusetts, it lasted six months. I saw some

Airborne soldiers in Boston and decided that is what I wanted to be and that is how I ended up in the Army at the age of sixteen as well. We fought in the coldest place U.S. troops have ever fought in, that brutal war in Korea. At the end of my enlistment, I enlisted into the Marine Corps. I spent most of my time with the 2nd Marine Division at Camp Lejeune, North Carolina, until my discharge date and then I enlisted into the Air Force. I retired with twenty-one years of active duty in 1968. Who knows better about those puddle hoppers than I?"

Bob said, "My father would always remind us of him being amongst good company as a Veteran of Underage Military Service." Gerard told us, "Several prominent members of the U.S. Congress have joined the military underage. Congressman Bob Stump of Arizona, Chairman of the House Armed Services Committee, served in the Navy at the age of sixteen. The late Congressman Joe Moakley of Massachusetts, former Chairman of the House Rules Committee, enlisted in the Navy at the age of fifteen and served in the South Pacific during World War II. He died Memorial Day 2001 after serving nearly thirty years as a member of Congress. Senator Mike Mansfield of Montana served as Majority Leader of the U.S. Senate longer than anyone before him, and later as Ambassador to Japan for twelve years. He joined the Navy at the age of fourteen, the Army at the age of fifteen, and the Marines at the age of seventeen. He died at the age of 98 in 2001."

Bob said, "Miguel, it is very interesting, to say the least, my dad may not remember much of what is going on today, asks the same questions over and over, tells the same stories over and over. The most amazing thing about it all is his behavior when he cannot remember where he put his eyeglasses. He gets so angry with himself or the world for not developing an eyeglasses finder, like the telephone finder button, so he would not have to spend so much time looking for his stupid glasses. This is every day. But he remembers every moment vividly on Hill 420 near Wonton-ni, Korea, that day in May 1941. To sit there and listen to my dad and his good friend Rudy Hernandez talk about it, moment by moment, thanking each other for saving their lives over and over with explanations, has to be shared with the world. You see, my dad was there when they noticed Rudy was still alive after he was about to be placed into the black bag as killed in action, but Dad also saw the slight movement of Rudy's hand. The medics confirmed and validated he was still with us. Rudy was lying among the bodies of six Koreans who had been killed during the combat. My father had so many stories to validate who he believes are real heroes. 'Not those fresh water sailors and puddle hoppers,' as he would say.

"I remember another story he shared about a crazy, patriotic thirteen-year-old who had joined the Marines illegally. This kid, Billy Trero, ran away from home and enlisted in Alabama, forging his birth date and parent's signature on his application. His first campaign was at Guadalcanal, one of the first major offensive decisive victories in the Pacific theater in World War II. During another battle, he took some shrapnel in the leg, but doctored himself in the field for fear of being shipped home. Billy had been honorably discharged after being shot in the leg during his third campaign of the war. It was alleged an American tank driver found him. He earned three Battle Stars and a Purple Heart for his service to the country, all before he turned seventeen years old. He was sent home twenty-one days shy of his seventeenth birthday, at which time most other young men were about to legally join the armed forces in WWII with their parents' consent. Billy was still restless after his discharge from the military. So he used the G.I. Bill and learned to fly. He joined the Merchant Marines, shipping ammunition over to the war zone. But most interestingly, he won the state Golden Gloves title in Alabama. He also won the Junior Olympics title in Houston—all by the time he was twenty-one years old. He turned pro and fought for nine years. According to my Dad, 'This is what real warriors do.'"

These shared stories do not in any way give credence to minimize the value of the contributions of the U.S. Coast Guard in keeping this nation strong, serving our citizens and the world, or the patriotism and commitment to world freedom by those Veterans of Underage Military Service members. Their legacies should live on as valuable chapters in our history.

I once read, "If our nation's fifth and smallest military service was a cutter it would be listed as severely crippled from the lack of political support and those words feared by any Guardian: 'the curse of can-do,' which results in an overwhelming workload. In the face of an impending budget cut and manpower reductions, the Coast Guard must confront severe challenges that threaten its performance and long-term viability, as it comports with the realities of the post-9/11 environment and the state of world affairs. What is to become of the world's best Coast Guard or will it take the path of Britain's Royal Navy, becoming a shadow of its former self?" I truly believe every word spoken, with great concerns for our younger generation and how the safety of this nation may be compromised.

As most great leaders would, Jeff attributes his career success to the men and women he served with and the empowerment the leaders in his chain of command had trusted him with. But he expressed his deep disappointment with the Veterans Affairs after retirement from the military. It is, without question, "no documentation; no service connected condition occurred." As with many military members, in an effort to protect their career, they would most likely self-medicate instead of seeking medical attention. The worst part of this scenario is the fact that the VA does not educate the veteran community on the possible presumptive service conditions, such as prostate cancer, diabetes, leukemia, Hodgkin's, Parkinson's, respiratory cancer, or the higher risk of birth defects as a result of the exposure to the herbicide Agent Orange. An acoustic trauma condition as a result of the occupational exposure while working around loud noises from weapons, aircrafts, engine rooms, etc., most likely would cause hearing loss and tinnitus. The duties of a Guardsman would definitely lend itself to acoustic traumatic conditions—not the perception of a spouse who believed she was being ignored when her husband simply couldn't hear her. Understandably Jeff was disappointed with the VA for the denial of his request for these conditions since there is no medical evidence to show the condition either occurred in or was caused by the service. Jeff said, "The crazy thing about being on a Coast Guard cutter is that I, as well as most of the Coasties, worked on the transmitter deck and in engine rooms which are very loud. The high level of radio frequency contamination is often ignored. The Record of Occupational Exposure disregarded the fact that those transmitters produced 275,000 rams of power. Also several veterans I served with came down with serious medical conditions as a result of exposure to radiation during their military service that was denied as service-connected. But after four or five years and hiring an attorney, the VA awarded them service-connected conditions. I have written buddy statements for a couple of veterans I served with. The veterans who do not have the money to pay for assistance oftentimes would die with their case pending.

"The large number of cases being processed, coupled with all kinds of delays, collecting the initial medical evidence submitted oftentimes takes more than a year, which necessitates an extra delay for the VA to schedule a compensation and pension examination to proceed with the processing. In that span of time several of my veteran friends have died. I was lucky, at the end of my twenty-seven-and-a-half-year career, I made a copy of my medical records and provided a copy to the VA to review and establish claims for those conditions I have that would be service-connected and I was granted twenty percent disability. There are lots of medical conditions that were omitted because I did not seek military medical attention for personal and professional reasons. I cannot and will not blame anyone but myself for this action."

Only with experiences as shared can the younger generation realize our legacies and the historical significance, with reminders of the struggles in our journey. I hope the people of this nation would find an effective method, to go before the world as a reminder of our veterans' sacrifices for the world's freedom of mankind. As well, as not to forget the secondary casualty sufferers—the spouses, children, and family members—who often suffer from a silent or hidden type of depression and PTSD conditions as a result of the veterans' service-connected conditions. These scars are a lot deeper than most people would imagine. Several family members explained how they have put their lives on hold to care for a veteran, parents, or sibling. A spouse may harbor silent anger while enduring sacrifices in their own careers, following the veteran around the world. Divorce drama is oftentimes traumatic for military families, but greater for a Coastie as it is such a small unit; everybody knows everything going on within the unit. Jeff said, "I had a three-year assignment to Group Key West, Florida, but after two years I was reassigned to an isolated tour, at LORST Saint Paul Island, Alaska, in the harsh Bering Sea." I cannot imagine what it was like for Jeff and his first spouse, Marge, after so many years of marriage when he got back from his isolated tour to be confronted with the divorce proceedings. Marge left the country with both their children to marry a Navy submarine sailor in Scotland. The drama did not stop with Jeff and Marge but both the kids may have accepted the blame, themselves. Jeff said, "I don't want to know or don't care to know what was going on during my isolated tour. The temptations coupled with loneliness can be overpowering and she fell in love. I was reassigned to Hawaii and promoted to Chief Petty Officer, but two of us were vying for one spot and I was assigned back overseas to the U.S. Coast Guard Far East section at the U.S. Embassy in Tokyo in 1989. This is where I met the most wonderful and perfect woman, I wanted to share a life with her forever. Sue and I were married after five years of knowing and appreciating each other. It has been the best thing I have ever done. Sue is my rock who keeps me grounded; she is everything to me; the world would be nothing without her in it. Most of the good things in my life have come since our acquaintance and subsequent marriage."

CHAPTER SIXTEEN

The Mom's Struggles with a Traumatic Brain Injured Son

"Some people live an entire lifetime and wonder if they
have ever made a difference in the world, but the
Marines don't have that problem."

– PRESIDENT RONALD REAGAN

"Every heart knows its own sorrow and the greatest casualty of war is to be forgotten," explain mothers and spouses of their journeys with their traumatic brain injured (TBI) veteran. These were some very heart-wrenching words to hear. "The journey is not a simple matter and definitely complicates our daily lives. It is like being on an emotional roller coaster, which is perhaps a simplistic way of encapsulating the daily journey," said one mother.

Despite the difficulties in locating the veteran, meeting Thomas and his mother Marie, turned out to be a transformational experience. At long last MapQuest guided me to their home and my first experience with a struggling mother's fight and challenges. The urgency of this visit was clearly directed from both congressional and senatorial interest for an Operation Iraqi Freedom and Operation Enduring Freedom (OIF/OEF) veteran. He was injured by sniper fire while serving in Fallujah, Iraq. During his recovery from a gunshot that had entered one leg and traveled into the other leg, he had contracted an infection in his bloodstream. The infection caused him to have anoxic brain damage that left him blind and paralyzed from the neck down, on life support, and in a vegetative state for five months. His mother said, "It was a hospital-borne infection that almost killed my child, called endocarditis, causing anoxic encephalopathy with cognitive deficits. I was not going to lose him again! My job is to use whatever means necessary to give him the best quality of life possible. As his mother, I have been his medical caregiver, coach, therapist, eyes, arms, legs, and all-around medical manager.

"Despite some initial medical prognosis after CT scans and MRIs, the doctors said there was no hope. He would either die or be severely brain damaged and not expected to wake up. A compassionate rehab doctor in San Diego said in confidence, 'If it were my son, I would get him to Doctor Scott in the Polytrauma Center at the VA Medical Center in Tampa, Florida.'" This Tampa Polytrauma Rehabilitation Center is one of four facilities in the country designed to provide intensive rehabilitative care to veterans and service members who have experienced severe injuries, including brain injuries, to more than one organ system. "It was amazing how quickly the chief of hospital services was able to make the arrangements after she made it clear she was well aware of the capabilities in Tampa. Thomas, my sister Betty, and I flew across the country in an Air Force medevac aircraft (an ambulance jet), from San Diego to Tampa."

Marie expressed her appreciation to finally have a face-to-face visit with someone from the VA fiduciary unit. She had made several telephone calls and sent e-mails with records she presented during the interview showing the number of attempts made, along with postal return receipts of letters mailed to the Regional Office. She surely welcomed this opportunity to express her frustration and anger with the VA's bureaucracy. It had forced her to seek assistance from both the senators and congressmen in Colorado and Florida. This was necessary because Thomas' home of records was Colorado and he is currently residing in Florida, clinging to life. Marie said, "It was a miracle. With the congressional and senatorial intervention, the VA started answering the mail, calling me, and now your visit. It is sad to believe he sacrificed his life for his country and we are fighting this type of battle for his benefits. It has taken these actions to get results. Especially when I reflect on how Thomas was found posturing and unresponsive in the medical holding room at the Naval Medical Center after going unnoticed for more than twenty hours. This is when he suffered the brain injury, caused by the infection resulting from treatment for the gunshot wounds. His struggle and my blessing has been the journey to get him better. But answering the mail in the benefits department is another battle. The legal community would not accept a case like this because my son was on active duty and the government cannot sue the government. He cannot sue the government because he was a member of the government during his mishaps. Thomas is my only child and the best friend a mother could ever dream of having, since he was born. For the VA to ignore us like just another number is unacceptable.

I am all he has and for the government to impose this unnecessary stress is totally wrong. I need to be strong for and with him. Weakness is not a choice or an available option in our world. Thomas is my world and I will do whatever it takes to ensure he enjoys the best things life offers.

"I vividly recall the evening I got the call," she said. "It was not clear at the time how urgent my visit to San Diego was, because I had tickets to go visit him in three days. The caller on the other end of the phone had urged me to get to California as soon as possible, 'the sooner the better,' he said. I was oblivious to the horror that loomed ahead.

"Thank God my flight left early enough with a stop in Denver. Both my sister and brother-in-law met me at the airport. My sister Betty, with only an ID and credit card in hand, purchased a plane ticket to accompany me to San Diego. It was a long flight. I knew in my heart and mind something was seriously wrong, not sure what, but kept my emotions under control. On the other hand Betty, who was my support, needed my support fearing bad news, with many tearful moments. Things got a little worse for her when we landed in San Diego and were met by the head chaplain and the commander of the San Diego Marine Division. She just totally lost it and I had to console her; therefore, my initial suspicions were correct. Something was seriously wrong, but I was able to manage my emotions by consoling my sister. Looking back, my sister's behavior was a distraction, which allowed me to brace myself for things to come. The greeting party at the hospital gave us a choice of seeing Thomas right away or meeting with the doctors first, and I agreed to see the doctors. A team of more than ten doctors, nurses, and specialists met with us in a private room. The briefing was so surreal, nothing close to what we had imagined. The chief of hospital services said, 'Thomas has suffered from an infection and had gone without oxygen for quite some time. He had also suffered from a series of strokes and had anoxic brain damage in combination with other disabling conditions and side effects, which they are not able to diagnose at this time. He was not awake, but on life-support machines.' Accepting the briefing first was the right choice, because when I saw my son for the first time he did not look like himself. His eyes were wide open, dilated, and his body oddly swollen, especially his hands. It was not the son I brought into this world, loved, and raised. I thought he appeared to be dying, which I refused to accept. Life was a blur during those days," Marie said. "I spent most of my time sitting next to my son with this inner voice telling me, 'together we WILL make it.' That voice was so powerful. Especially watching him on the life-support system for fifteen long days. Then the medical team had to do an emergency extubation as a result of his breathing tube clogging from his pneumonia. The choice was to either reintubate or trachea him. I said no to the tracheotomy, because I believed he would not have wanted to live like that.

"At his side during those dreadful five months, watching him barely clinging to life, in a vegetative state, the prognosis the doctors and specialists provided was painful. I held on to hope and that inner voice. I reflected on the deals we made, wondering if my being a two-time divorcée with an expectation of getting married to the man I was dating and Thomas walking me down the aisle were retribution for not doing things right. It was a mental blame game with me. I also wondered if I was being punished for something I could or should have done differently. Being a single parent with a dropout son from a school we believed to have been the worst high school in our community, I had made a deal with Thomas to obtain his GED. He passed the GED exam with flying colors and started taking college courses in between working at a restaurant until the 9/11 attacks. Thomas enlisted into the Marines as his moral obligation to America. This was shocking to us all because no one in our family had ever served in the military. I could not have been any prouder of my son the day I witnessed his graduation from boot camp in San Diego in December 2005. The guilt of me failing or not doing the right things as a single parent had subsided. Thomas' lifelong plan was to be a police officer. He had enrolled in pre-law and was doing an internship with a San Diego medical malpractice attorney who had become a mentor and a good friend. Thomas had such a magnetic personality that most people gravitated to him. The proof of his personality was noted during his hospitalization in San Diego, when many family members and friends visited to provide Thomas with all the love, comfort, and support one could possibly have. With the dreadful journey of uncertainty, I did not waver in my strong belief Thomas was still with us and determined to prove the doctors wrong."

Marie said, "I will never forget the day in April when he said his first words. I had been torturing him with his favorite comedies, *South Park* and *Family Guy*, as a therapeutic means of communication. For some reason I suspected Thomas could hear and understand, but was unable to move his body. I also remembered a few days after his brain injury, while in the intensive care unit on life support, a group of his fellow Marines were in his room visiting him. His gunny sergeant, with his booming voice, was talking about how Thomas' fellow Marine, the man who found him unconscious in his room, was 'getting so fat that the only thing he could get by when he walked down the halls was the paint on the wall.'

Everyone in the room started laughing. The very corners of my son's mouth were tilted up, he was laughing. I knew in my heart, my son was still with us, he could hear and understand, but something would not allow him to communicate his thoughts. I promised him I would not give up." The conviction in her voice and sense of gratification was indescribable as she went on sharing the moment. She said, "It had appeared to me, he was somewhat agitated and restless, but did not communicate his feelings. I had just taken him back to his hospital room and asked him, "Do you want to watch *Family Guy* or *South Park*? *South Park*?" I was astonished and overcome by emotions when Thomas said, 'NO.' I cried out in excitement, 'thank the Lord,' but maintained my faculties and grabbed my camera, and recorded the next few words. I said, 'Say Mom.' He said, 'Mom.' By this time I was crying, screaming with joy, and had been joined by all the nurses and other family members up on 5 North at the James Haley VA Medical Center, Tampa Polytrauma Unit. Words could never express this joy. My son could speak again! Most people in the room were also crying with shared joy for us, personal gratification for the care they rendered to my son in allowing this to happen, or for the families who hope a miracle of some kind would bless them."

Marie said she was adamant about getting Thomas out of the hospital as soon as possible to avoid further hospital-borne infections, which caused him to be in the predicament he was now in. "We have come too far to lose him now." She had gotten married to the man she was dating before Thomas was injured and relocated to the Tampa area to continue with the outstanding medical treatment Thomas was receiving. She was not too pleased with the VA Benefits Department, but very appreciative of the continuous medical care rendered.

She apologized for her bitterness, anger, disappointment, and lack of trust in the VA Benefits System as she attempted to validate her behavior by saying, "The VA granted my son service-connected disabilities with the effective date of October 2008 after his discharge from the U.S. Marine Corps that September. Funds could not be released until I was appointed fiduciary payee within 45 days from March 27, 2009. This is the day I was visited by the VA Fiduciary Field Examiner. It was only because my son's case had senatorial and congressional intervention. I am grateful to all those who made it possible, but wonder about those warriors who do not have that type of support. We had purchased a four-bedroom, three-bath single-family dwelling after his release from the Tampa Polytrauma Rehab Center for continuing care." Marie said, "I found it incomprehensible for this organization to be so oblivious of the veterans' personal and psychological issues such as pain, depression, insomnia, substance abuse, and the total dependency on others when a caregiver is required 24/7, instead of being so entrenched in the total control of the estate protection, without regard to the humane requirements. I do understand the concerns for fraud, misuse, and abuse when it is warranted, but I am unable to understand the undue harassment from the VA Fiduciary Unit.

"What good is money in the bank for a veteran who is legally blind and paralyzed from the neck down, when no one can use the money in his best interest?" was the rhetorical question Marie asked with conviction. She also described the fiduciary unit's inconsistency as dysfunctional: "Three different field examiners in three years with three different management philosophies, and the consolidation of the legal instrument examiner functional responsibilities in the South Carolina Hub, are insane. Being legally, morally, and ethically responsible to my son, the VA fiduciary is a badly broken system, nothing but a non-customer focused entity. The intimidating assault by the VA with idle threats to suspend the benefits and removal as the fiduciary payee for the veteran benefits is preposterous." She said, "I don't have a life. I live with and for my son every day. I will do whatever it takes to care and serve my son as I would my God."

It was our second meeting after five years. Marie had a laundry list of flustering, distressing, and depressing issues she had been battling with the VA fiduciary unit, all catalogued in a three-ring binder. She attributes the root cause of those stressful moments to the fallacies in the first budget we established without knowledge or historical wisdom of her son's future needs. The VA flaunted an overly aggressive, bullying approach, which seemed unnecessarily burdensome. It worries her, she said, "because I often think of the alternative. The thought of my son in a VA nursing home as just another number or patient with such demands means no one would have time for him. Those thoughts cause anxiety attacks and I pray to God to allow me the strength to fight a good fight," as she held back her tears.

In an effort to control her emotions and change focus, she opened her big binder with all the correspondence between her and the VA. Marie's administrative skills were ones to be emulated. It had an index with tabs and source documents to support the issues addressed. The first thing in the binder was a letter of admonishment from the VA fiduciary unit for Thomas' two trips to the Dominican Republic for stem cell treatments, which had restored his partial vision. She did not have prior approval. The letter stated her failure to ascertain prior approval could be deemed as fraud and misuse of funds. She said, "The sad thing about my son having money in the bank is to be able to pay a few hundred dollars to purchase a Corporate Surety Insurance Bond to protect funds over $150,000." She showed me another harsh letter for purchasing a generator without authorization or requested permission, while their home was experiencing blackouts during a hurricane, and for having the garage door repaired. She had addressed both these issues as emergencies. Marie stated her frustration, "My son is paralyzed from the neck down, and is wheelchair-bound with several medical complications that require electrical power. The garage is his main entrance or exit from the house. Going around to the back entrance is hard with the electrical wheelchair; in an emergency, we'd use the garage door." She challenged them to prove she did not request permission; no one answered the phone nor returned her calls. The telephone records showed she had placed calls to the VA number around those days. Marie also had a letter requesting permission to get an estimate to renovate the front door to be wheelchair-accessible, which was never answered.

Among several letters and source documents in her binder were a couple of letters she called, "the VA sledge hammer." These were the VA fiduciary accounting disapproval letters. Marie said, "It was clear, the reviewer does not have the sense of a reasonable person. In between those figures is a human being with unusual but reasonable needs who absolutely cannot do things for himself and requires total care. He can remove his eyeglasses with his left hand with some difficulty, and I try to comply with the rules, which are so ambiguous.

"For example, the first disapproval letter I received stated, 'Your accounting was disapproved for the following: 1.

You did not account for the Social Security funds.' But in accordance with the fiduciary agreement I signed, it was for VA-derived funds. I have to submit a separate accounting to Social Security and I don't understand the redundancy. '2. You did not receive prior approval for the following expenses which were items clearly listed on your properly titled bank statement.' Each of the items was clearly addressed with footnotes and explanations. '3. Your items on the bank statement list exceed the $1,000 established limitation.' I was authorized for a $1,200 incidental/miscellaneous allowance. '4. The present accounting is also disapproved as a result of your two previous years accounting being disapproved along with several other aggravating issues.' This is when Marie lost it because she had submitted the documents; the legal instrument examiner put the documents in the files without actions and never replied to her either way. Marie claimed to have forwarded a detailed letter with all her documents to both her Republican and Democratic senators and congressmen with pictures of her son prior to deployment and now sitting in his wheelchair, requesting their assistance. Three days later she had two legal instrument examiners from the VA fiduciary unit and their supervisor knocking on her door. Marie said, "We spent hours going over every document in the binder, item by item, substantiating evidence to support the noted discrepancies, to include the ledger in the computer and validate her inability to obtain data from the Social Security records. Our meeting really showed the fiduciary unit record-keeping system was broken, but the supervisor was stuck on me using VA funds at the local gentlemen's club as misuse. I beg to differ and questioned her opinion of having a 25-year-old son whose mind and physical needs are still active. The only thing he wanted for his birthday was to visit a gentlemen's club. Because my husband refused to take Thomas to such an establishment, I had no choice but to take him. It was not a comfortable decision or good experience for me to watch half-naked women shaking their breasts in my son's face, improvising a lap dance, and he having the time of his life. However, I could not help but wonder if he could also have blood flow necessary in other areas. I questioned the supervisor, 'What should I do? Or how would you manage such a special commanding request on such a special occasion? But before you answer these questions, please look at my son and then explain to me your answer.' I showed a picture of my son during his first fifteen days on life support, which I would often use to reflect on our blessing. She never answered, other than to say, 'not to use VA funds.' It was obvious we had a communication breakdown. The VA fiduciary unit had taken the power control approach, which was not what I believe to have been the intent of Congress when the fiduciary laws were established. I am sure a convict with a long rap sheet would have been treated with more dignity or as a human being if the IRS were reviewing their case. The 'you do as I say approach' is the standard business practice the fiduciary unit offers their customers.

"The constant battles with intimidating tactics, being bullied, and inconsistencies are undue emotional stressors I often endure. This distracts from the required attention and care Thomas demands daily. I try my best to shelter him from the distractions because he would become so out of control. He bites himself, screams at the top of his voice with profanities, and cries uncontrollably blaming himself and everyone for his inabilities. It is so sad and terrifying at the same time." She did her best to avoid this type of behavior as much as possible, Marie said. The expression on her face, in sharing her conviction to protect her son at any cost, was that of a mama bear's face if someone or something messed with her cub.

It took me back to the first time I met with Marie and Thomas during the initial field examination. I could not help but marvel at this mother's devotion in putting her son's needs first, above everything in her life. She said, "My son offered his life for the freedom of this country and the least I could do is to give it back to him." The most amazing thing about the meeting was his courage and belief he was a miracle child and would get better. Thomas said, "Mr. Miguel, my condition is only a stopping place in my journey of life and I know I will get better." He kept reaffirming how much he loved his mother and stating she was the best mother God put on this earth. Marie said, "He may not be able to do the things he used to do, the way he did them, but it does not mean he is worse. It means our life is different and we are blessed. Thomas is grateful to God for allowing him to still be with us to witness the first black president of the United States and for Tim Tebow to take the Denver Broncos to the playoffs." She had to show me her first, second, and third letters she received from her son during his boot camp training and read each one out loud. She said, "These are treasured memories." The look on her face was priceless, the tone of her voice made the hair on my arms stand at attention.

It has been five years into their emotional roller coaster journey. Adapting, adjusting, and recovering are the lifeline in making it through each day, Marie said. She admitted to having lain in bed for three-and-a-half years, crying with joy or sadness, because God's plans were not the dream she had for her son or future grandchildren, or how crazy life would be for her son if something would happen to her. Every morning during her devotions she asks God for another miracle in Thomas' life, a new medical discovery or miracle. At the end of each day when nothing happens, she cries, but still thanks God for the strength to keep hope alive. She reads every available medical scientific study on traumatic brain injuries or "How Adult Stem Cells are Transforming Medicine around the World." She submitted her son's case as a candidate for cell transplantation in a severe brain injury study conducted in Russia. Thomas was unable to make the long trip because he was hospitalized twice with pulmonary complications. She is well aware of the world's evidence-based outcomes in brain stem science and hopes one day her son will be a success story in a medical journal. She admits, VA medicine has been remarkable, but conceded to the fact of them having done all science and the law will allow them to do, which is not enough to be acceptable to her.

"The healthy son born to me is gone, but I still have my son I care for and love more each day than the day before. The reason and motive for this deep love is different. He was my joy, best friend, and dream, but now I am his caregiver, his everything, and our hope," Marie said, "I loved who he was and prayed every day in every situation for his protection with the covering of the blood of Jesus. I hoped for grandchildren and a happy marriage for him. Since the traumatic brain injury, my prayers are much simpler. I am grateful to God for the blessing to have spared his life and ask for a medical miracle." She described her state of being as, "an unambiguous grief, a grief that goes on and on without clarity." She believes it is worse than those loved ones whose relative has been declared missing in action (MIA) and they never receive their remains. They don't have closure, as she has daily concerns about her son's outcome, but still physically has his presence. She has learned to love and accept Thomas as her world.

Postlude

A military burial service is truly impressive and memorable for the people attending, especially the younger generation who may witness such an event for the first time. The hearse door is opened to reveal a flag-draped coffin. Silently, except for the tap of their polished shoes on the pavement, a group of seven in the honor guard makes its way to their fallen comrade. With precision, six of them retrieve the coffin from the hearse in three movements. We sense that they see this as a rescue of sorts. They recognize this as a fallen comrade who is not yet at rest, and who will not be until they make it so. With the casket safely in hand, the six escorts slowly march toward the hallowed ground that has been prepared to receive their comrade. When the flag-draped carrier is place above its final resting place, the six remove the flag and hold it tightly in their white-gloved hands over the casket, while the seventh, too, stands near. They all stand guard, at alert attention, over the grave until the guardsman in the distance who holds the silver sword directs his charge to honor the fallen one with the ultimate military salute.

On his command, the remaining seven present their arms and each fires simultaneously, three times, comprising a salute of twenty-one guns. After the sound of the gunfire, it is replaced with the mournful, most familiar of military melodies, *Taps*.

The honor guard ceremonially folds the American flag. The highest-ranking officer presents the folded flag to the family with a brief statement of gratitude and a salute. The only person remaining at the grave is one soldier, the vigil. His mission is to watch over the body until it is interred into the ground.

It is clear in my mind this is how I want to be honored when it is my day to meet with my maker.

About the Author

M iguel Reece is a military veteran with more than thirty years of service in the United States Air Force, both as an enlisted member (Technical Sergeant/E-6) and an officer (Major/O-4), with an additional ten years with the Department of Veterans Affairs Regional Office, St. Petersburg, Florida. He is a Vietnam veteran who served in Phu Cat Air Base, Plei Ku Air Base, and Tuy Hoa Air Base. He was drafted into the U.S. Army December 1968, but left Michigan and enlisted into the U.S. Air Force in February 1969. He continued his education after his friends, Jimmy Sims and Tyrone Valentine, persisted on the value of an education for a young black man in the military and the world, for that matter. Miguel earned two Associate of Science degrees (City College of Chicago and The University of New York, Albany), a Bachelor of Science in Education (Southern Illinois University), and Master's of Arts degree in Procurement and Acquisition, which opened several important doors with great challenges and opportunities in his life.

Miguel served in Vietnam and went on to support Desert Storm, was an Administrator on the State Department-Sponsored Humanitarian and Civic Action Mission to Jordan, was the Support Commander of the Field Integration of the Air Transportable Hospital deployed to Cairo, Egypt, in "Bright Star," and served on the Stabilization Team, with the Expeditionary Medical Forces, in the Balkans. These experiences have provided Miguel with a holistic regard for the honor and veneration which the veterans of the United States Armed Forces and families merit. As we stood guard for the freedom of America, and the world, we must continue to recognize and appreciate how the veterans have kept the world safe for democracy.

Retirement after thirty years in the United States Air Force, having lived in or visited twenty-nine countries in the world, posed new challenges for Miguel. After eighteen months of playing golf and visiting friends around the world, he continued to wait on the rating decision for the service-connected disabilities he had applied for prior to his retirement. The AMVETS Veterans Service Representative who had been assisting Miguel with his claim suggested that Miguel apply for employment with the Department of Veterans Affairs. Making a difference is Miguel's aspiration and working for the Veterans Affairs would be a perfect fit.

It truly saddened Miguel the day he announced his retirement for medical reasons. Being a public servant and making a difference in the lives of the beneficiaries, had been an unconditional love Miguel shared for his job, the privilege of serving the veterans, and working more than half of the counties in the state of Florida. He visited veterans and/ or their families where they lived—under bridges, in a tree house, in parks, nursing homes, assisted-living facilities, and fabulous homes—everywhere Miguel believed it is their right to be treated with dignity and class. The reminiscences and experiences of the veterans and their families, coupled with Miguel's concerns, are such treasured memories he felt he would be remiss in not sharing their stories with the world.